JESUS THE PACIFIST

A Concise Guide to His Radical Nonviolence

Matthew Curtis Fleischer

Epic Octavius the Triumphant, LLC
Oklahoma City, OK

Published by Epic Octavius the Triumphant, LLC
Oklahoma City, OK

First Edition 2020

ISBN 978-0-9994306-2-0 (paperback)

Printed in the United States of America

Line editing by Christinah Mulder.
Copy editing by Susan Dimmock.
Cover design by Christian Fuenfhausen.

www.MatthewCurtisFleischer.com

CONTENTS

FOREWORD

A number of years ago I was a guest on a Christian radio talk show. The host and I talked for thirty minutes or so about how Christians often get too caught up in politics and nationalism, and the discussion seemed to go very well. The host then opened up the line for call-in questions. The first call was a question about whether or not I thought Christians should serve their country by fighting in and supporting the military. I responded by pointing out that both Jesus and Paul instructed us to swear off all violence and to instead love, pray for, and do good to our enemies. I explained that, while I don't judge Christians who enlist in the armed forces, I personally could not see how a person could genuinely love and do good to their enemies when they were, at the same time, trying to kill them.

There was a brief but intensely awkward silence when I finished. "Wow," my host finally exclaimed, still live on the radio. "You could just feel the air get sucked out of the room when Boyd said that!" And then, my host and his entire audience (so it seemed) turned on me.

The next call was from a vet who had lost a close friend while fighting in Iraq. "My friend was as Christian as they come," this angry caller said,

> and he gave his life for the God and the blessed country he believed in. My buddy was willing to make the ultimate sacrifice to protect your freedom, including your freedom to get on the air and say whatever is on your mind, like you're doing right now. Yet you have the audacity to publicly return his favor by suggesting that he shouldn't have been fighting over there in the first place!

I gently reminded this caller that I was sharing my own perspective, not judging his friend or anyone else. I also pointed out that a person such as myself can appreciate the sacrifice soldiers are willing to make, even though their own religious convictions prevent them from participating in the military or any other office that might require them to harm or kill another human.

I then asked this caller how he interpreted Jesus's instruction to "love your enemies and pray for those who persecute you, so that you may be children of your Father in heaven." In a voice that quivered with rage, he replied,

1

Well, I don't know. But I'll tell you this: whatever Jesus meant when he referred to enemies that we're supposed to love, he sure as hell wasn't talking about enemies like ISIS! The only way to handle evil enemies like this is to blow them away in the name of the Lord!

Seemingly energized by this caller, the host then chimed in, saying that since the majority of soldiers identify as Christian, if all American Christian soldiers heeded my interpretation of Jesus's words, America would in short order be overrun with Islamic terrorists and we'd all be under Sharia law. "Do you think *that* would be God's will?" he asked in a sarcastic voice. His question seemed to further ignite the anger of his audience toward me, and the next twenty minutes of responding to hostile callers was not a pleasant experience!

My experience on this Christian talk show illustrates one of the main reasons so few American Christians take seriously Jesus's (and Paul's) instruction to abstain from all violence and to instead love and bless our enemies. It just doesn't make sense! Sure, we can all agree that we should love enemies like our grouchy neighbors, our nasty bosses, and perhaps even our ornery in-laws. But to most American Christians, any suggestion that God would actually want his people to refrain from using whatever force was necessary to protect their loved ones and their country is met with disbelief and anger. It "sucks the air right out of the room."

In reality, these are exactly the kinds of enemies Jesus was talking about! When a first-century Jew living in Roman-occupied Palestine spoke of an "enemy" to a Jewish audience, the first thing that would pop into the minds of most people would be *the Romans*. The Romans ruled the lands they conquered through terror, and Palestine was no different. If a group caused them problems, as various first-century Jewish groups sometimes did, Romans often responded by sending a battalion of soldiers into the town where the families of the trouble-makers likely lived to randomly seize a number of people and crucify them on a nearby hillside. "If you mess with us," the Romans were saying, "this is what happens to you and your loved ones."

Consequently, most Jews despised the Romans at least as much as most Americans despise terrorist groups today, except that in the case of first-century Jews, the Roman terrorists had *already conquered*. They were living under a foreign rule of law that was as offensive to

Jews as Sharia law would be to the vast majority of Americans today. Yet, Jesus had the audacity to instruct his followers that they are to love, bless, and do good to *these kinds of enemies*! The kinds of enemies who ruthlessly kill your loved ones, just to terrorize you and everyone else into submission.

In short, when Jesus commands us to love enemies, it includes the worst sort of enemies imaginable—i.e., terrorists.

If this offends you, brace yourself for worse. For not only did Jesus instruct his audience to love the terrorists who ruled over them, he went on to add that we are to love our enemies like this "*that you may be* children of your Father in heaven; for he makes his sun rise on the evil and on the good, and sends rain on the righteous and on the unrighteous" (Matt. 5:44-45). In other words, Jesus makes loving the worst sort of enemy imaginable the pre-condition for being considered a child of the Father. The Father loves like the sun shines and the rain falls: indiscriminately. And we put on display that we have the Father's life in us when we love *like that*: the evil and the wicked along with the good.

And lest anyone suspect that this is an isolated "difficult" teaching of Jesus that stands in tension with the rest of the New Testament, quite the opposite is the case. As Fleischer powerfully demonstrates in the book you're now reading, Jesus's teaching on non-violence (actually, on *anti*-violence, as Fleischer makes clear) and on loving enemies permeates his teachings and the teachings of the New Testament authors, and it lies at the heart of Jesus's own exemplary life and death.

We thus find ourselves in this awkward situation. On the one hand, loving enemies and being committed to anti-violence lies at the heart of the gospel and is the tell-tale indicator that one is "a child of the Father in heaven." But, on the other hand, the majority of American Christians, following the dominant Church tradition since the fourth century, don't take this teaching seriously because it just doesn't conform to their common sense. They are thus generally content to adopt the attitude of the caller who insisted that, whatever Jesus meant "by those enemies we're supposed to love, he sure as hell didn't meant enemies like ISIS."

In this easy-to-read and compellingly argued book, Fleischer masterfully demonstrates that this attitude is simply not an option for the committed follower of Jesus. Among other things, Fleischer carefully considers every possible objection to Jesus's pacifism, whether they are rooted in common sense or in a particular reading of Scripture, and demonstrates that they simply do not stand up to scrutiny. And if this radical teaching fails to conform to our common sense, that should hardly surprise us, since the "common sense" of most Americans is grounded in the myth of redemptive violence, in American exceptionalism, and in a host of other assumptions that are at odds with Jesus's vision of the kingdom of God. Moreover, we are followers of a God who displayed his omnipotence and his wisdom by letting himself get crucified (1 Cor. 1:18, 24). If this reveals anything about God, it's that God does not conform to our notions of common sense!

If you are not yet convinced that loving enemies and being committed to anti-violence lies at the heart of the Good News, I challenge you to read this book. Even if it fails to completely convince you, it will at the very least force you to think through your position more rigorously, which is always a good thing. But even if you are already a convinced pacifist, I encourage you to read this book. You will find in this tightly packed volume a treasure trove of insights that cannot help but strengthen your own pacifist convictions.

– Gregory A. Boyd

INTRODUCTION

If you are like most modern Christians, you have your doubts about Jesus's pacifism. You're aware he wasn't a violent revolutionary, generally preached against violence, and said some rather flowery things about turning the other cheek and loving your enemies. But you also know he cleared the temple with a whip, told his disciples to buy swords, praised a Roman centurion, frequently spoke of violent judgment, and will—according to Revelation—return one day to kill God's enemies with a sword. You've likely engaged with bits and pieces of the issue here and there, but you've never given it the focused, sustained attention necessary to reconcile the apparent contradictions.

This book attempts to remedy that. It provides a systematic, biblically based, comprehensive overview of Jesus's life and teachings on the subject of violence.

But why should you care? Why expend energy exploring Jesus's relationship with violence? Two reasons.

First, Jesus is our moral standard. As discussed at length in my previous book *The Old Testament Case for Nonviolence*, the Bible indicates on every level that we are to *obey* Jesus—not Moses or the God of the Old Testament.[1] Likewise, it declares that we are to *mimic* Jesus, not the ancient Israelites, Yahweh, or the God of the end times. Jesus, and Jesus alone, is our ethical ideal, our moral compass, the perfect example of how to do God's will on earth. Everything and everyone in the Bible declares it. Consequently, all justification for violence must come from his life and teachings, and nothing else.

Second, as this book demonstrates, nonviolence is central to Jesus's ethical teachings. It is not merely one of many minor peripheral moral issues he treats. Nor is it only for the particularly devout or merely a matter of personal conscience. It is a fundamental aspect of Christian discipleship, a necessary component of fulfilling God's will for our lives. As Walter Wink puts it, "nonviolence is not a fringe concern" but "the essence of the gospel," so essential that "Jesus's nonviolent followers should not be called pacifists, but simply Christians."[2]

Unfortunately, Jesus wasn't as explicit about violence as he could have been. He didn't unequivocally denounce all violence as always and everywhere immoral, nor did he provide us with a comprehensive list of acceptable and unacceptable uses. But that doesn't mean his stance on violence was vague. It wasn't. He gave us plenty of violence-related material to work with—material that, when carefully analyzed, yields a few clear, largely indisputable conclusions regarding the ethics of violence. Performing such an analysis is the task of this book.

Before we dive in, two definitions are in order. When I refer to *violence*, I mean the use of (unwelcome) physical force against a person or their property. In other words, I mean it in the relatively narrow, traditional sense, not in the broader, more modern sense of any action that causes any type of physical or nonphysical (verbal, psychological, spiritual, structural, cultural, etc.) harm. Actions that cause the latter types of harm are often as destructive as those that cause physical harm, but they are not our concern here. We are talking about direct physical actions like vandalism, theft, assault, kidnapping, rape, killing, war, and similar tangible acts of coercion, rather than things like insults, income disparities, greed, or racism, which alone are relatively indirect and nonphysical.

By *pacifism*, I mean the practice of nonviolence in all situations. I don't mean doing nothing. As you will see, Christian pacifism isn't passive. Like Jesus, it actively combats evil. It just does so nonviolently. It engages in nonviolent resistance, not nonresistance.

A word of warning: If you are not already a pacifist, this book will challenge you. You will likely think it goes too far in some spots. A few parts may even anger you. Most assuredly, you will not agree with all of it. I'm not asking you to. I'm asking you to give it a hearing, to allow its Jesus-centered case for radical nonviolence to enter your consciousness.

Of course, I hope you are persuaded by the evidence this book presents and the logic it employs. But if nothing else, I pray it is sufficiently sincere, rational, and biblically based to at least make Christian pacifism a more understandable position—even if you still don't adopt it.

---

[1] See Chapter 9, which makes this point from both a historical and theological perspective, backed up by a plethora of Scripture references.

[2] Walter Wink, *Engaging the Powers* 25th Anniversary Edition (Minneapolis, MN: Fortress Press, 2017), 232.

CHAPTER 1

JESUS'S GREATEST COMMAND: LOVE

In these first three chapters, we will analyze the role of violence in Jesus's teachings. We'll begin in this chapter with his greatest command, move to his other core teachings in Chapter 2, and then conclude with his most commonly misinterpreted sayings in Chapter 3.

Christian Ethics in One Word

Through Jesus, God has essentially given us just one command: to love. More specifically, he[1] has commanded us to love two things: him and our fellow humans. Here is Jesus's summation:

"Teacher, which is the greatest commandment in the Law?"

Jesus replied: "'Love the Lord your God with all your heart and with all your soul and with all your mind.' This is the first and greatest commandment. And the second is like it: 'Love your neighbor as yourself.' All the Law and the Prophets hang on these two commandments." (Matt. 22:36-40)[2]

That's it. That is all of God's commands summed up in just two: to love God and to love others.[3] All other commands merely clarify what it means to do those two things.[4] As Paul—considered by many to be Jesus's greatest interpreter—put it, "love is the fulfillment of the law" (Rom. 13:10).[5] It binds all other virtues "together in perfect unity" (Col. 3:14).

As Christians then, our sole duty is to love. To reference Paul again, we don't owe anyone anything but love.[6] Love is simultaneously the only thing God commands and all the things God commands. And in this sense, sin is failing to love. It is any and every unloving act (or failure to act).

The significance of love in Christianity is impossible to overstate. "Love is so central to Christian faith," writes Mildred Bangs Wynkoop, "that to touch it is to find oneself entangled with every element of Christian doctrine and life."[7]

For example, the Bible stresses an intrinsic and inseparable connection between God and love. It says that God is the source of love; we can't know God unless we love; we can't live in God or have God live in us unless we love; we must love in order to abide with God in eternity; love is why God sent Jesus to earth; and even that God is love.[8] Note the last point. Love is not merely an attribute of God. God doesn't just possess or express perfect love. God *is* love. Love is his very essence.

The Bible also tells us love is greater than even faith.[9] As Wynkoop explains, "it is not faith that satisfies the law, but it is love that is the fulfillment of the whole law…. Faith comes into its moral significance in love."[10] Or as James wrote, "What good is it, my brothers and sisters, if someone claims to have faith but has no deeds? … faith by itself, if it is not accompanied by [loving] action, is dead" (James 2:14, 17). According to Paul, *nothing* matters without love, not our spiritual gifts, not our biblical knowledge, not our charitable donations, and not even our faith.[11] "The only thing that counts," he wrote, "is faith *expressing itself through love*" (Gal. 5:6). Similarly, it is love, not faith, that conquers all.[12] Faith is essential, of course, but ultimately it is a means to the end of love.

As Christians, our purpose is to love. When we love, we obey God, do his will, advance his kingdom, satisfy our ethical obligations, and fulfill the reason for our being. After all, Jesus said the world would know his followers by their love. Not by their beliefs, their doctrines, their holiness, their piety, their prosperity, their popularity, or their power.[13] By their love.

In Christianity, love is everything. It is the gospel, the good news, and the goal of life. And it always has been, since the beginning.[14] In fact, it isn't going too far to declare that Christianity is love.

Defining Christian Love

So if the concept of love encapsulates all of Christian ethics, what precisely is Christian love? The Bible's most famous, precise, and comprehensive[15] definition of love describes it as patient, kind, non-envious, non-boastful, humble, honoring, selfless, not easily angered, forgiving, protecting, trusting, hopeful, persevering, and truthful.[16] The Bible's most detailed description of love in action says it is sincere, honors others above yourself, serves, is patient in affliction, shares with those in need, practices hospitality, blesses those who persecute you, lives in harmony with others, doesn't repay evil for evil, strives to live at peace with everyone, doesn't take revenge, provides care for enemies, and overcomes evil with good.[17] Likewise, according to the Bible's most well-known commands, the Ten Commandments, God-honoring love doesn't murder, doesn't commit adultery, doesn't steal, doesn't bear false witness, doesn't covet, and honors parents.[18]

The biblical lists of virtues and vices paint a similar picture. The virtues that describe Christian love include faith, hope, charity, joy, peace, patience, humility, kindness, compassion, generosity, mutual affection, perseverance, faithfulness, forgiveness, gentleness, self-control, and knowledge.[19] On the other hand, the vices that describe the opposite of Christian love include lust, gluttony, greed, sloth, wrath, envy, pride, lying, slander, hate, jealousy, thievery, drunkenness, devising wicked schemes, bearing false witness, rushing into evil, stirring up conflict, sexual immorality, and selfish ambition.[20]

The Bible also defines love as self-love. Most of the verses that command us to love others include the provision that we love them *as we love ourselves.*[21] So what does that mean?

I'm partial to C. S. Lewis's explanation in *Mere Christianity.* He contends we love ourselves by always wishing the best for ourselves. We don't always feel fond of or affection toward ourselves, enjoy our own company, or think we are a good person. We often hate the bad things we do, are sad we do them, and regret being the type of person who does them. Sometimes, we even understand our need for discipline and punishment. However, we continue hoping for and seeking our own ultimate good.

Stated another way, we all love ourselves by always seeking our own happiness. We all want food when we are hungry, a drink when we are thirsty, clothes when we are cold, comfort when we are hurting, and company when we are lonely. We all want to be safe, healthy, fulfilled, and loved. (Unfortunately, our sinful nature and ignorance often cause us to seek happiness in counterproductive and self-destructive ways, but that doesn't change the fact that we still wish good for ourselves.)

Therefore, to love others as we love ourselves is to treat them in this same way—to wish for and pursue their ultimate good, to promote their well-being like we promote our own. We don't have to feel fond of them, enjoy their company, or think they are nice when they are not. We don't have to ignore their sins or refrain from punishing them when they harm others. But we must always seek the best for them. That's how we love ourselves and how God loves us.

To view it another way, Christian love is the Golden Rule. It requires that we treat others as we want to be treated. Jesus himself even phrased it this way: "Do to others as you would have them do to you" (Luke 6:31).[22]

Most importantly, *Christ*ian love is *Christ*likeness. In the life and teachings of Jesus Christ, God has provided us with a perfect human example of how to love Christianly. The Bible explicitly and repeatedly commands us to love *like Jesus* loved and taught us to love.[23] He came to earth out of love and for love. Like Christianity itself, Jesus is love. Thus, Christian love is not simply an ideal, an abstract notion, a set of principles, or a list of commands. Christian love is a person.

That, my friends, is Christian love in a nutshell. Before we examine what it says about violence, let's refine our definition by exploring how it differs from secular conceptions of love.

Christian Love vs. Secular Love

In secular society today, love has a variety of meanings. Love can be a romantic feeling about another human being, as in "I'm in love with her." Love can be the physical sensation of sexual intercourse, as in "We made love." Love can be a non-romantic, surface-level affection for something, as in "I love the Yankees." Or love can be a deeper, more intimate non-romantic affection for someone, as occurs between friends or family members.

Christian love is none of these things. It is not a physical sensation, a romantic feeling, or a mutual emotional connection. It is not simply liking something in some pleasurable or sentimental way. It is not merely friendship or shared affection. It is much more beautiful than that.

For starters, while secular love is conditional, Christian love is unconditional. Secular love requires that someone be likable or provide us with something in return for our love. Christian love does not. It has no prerequisites and asks nothing in return. It loves not because someone is amiable, loves us back, or can give us something we want, but because God first loved us while we were unlikable and unloving and unable to provide him with anything in return.[24] It loves because God *continues* to love such people, even those who persecute him.[25] It bases its love on God's nature, not our fallen one.

Whereas secular love is often exclusive, Christian love is all-inclusive. Secular love excludes those who don't "qualify" (i.e., people we deem unworthy of our affection, including those who don't like us, don't treat us well, or who aren't part of our social tribe). Christian love excludes no one. The Bible commands us to love our neighbor and then defines our neighbor as *everyone*, even our enemy.[26]

While emotions drive secular love, thoughts drive Christian love. Christian love is a choice, a conscious and voluntary decision. It is not how you feel inside but what you think and intend. It is a mindset, not a sentiment. It is a commitment, not an affection. As C. S. Lewis put it, "Christian Love, either towards God or towards man, is an affair of the will" and "not of the feelings."[27] Or as Martin Luther King, Jr. quipped, "The meaning of [Christian] love is not to be confused with some sentimental outpouring. Love is something much deeper than emotional bosh."[28]

This is not to say that Christian love can't or doesn't produce good feelings. It can and does. But it isn't those feelings. And those feelings aren't the goal. Feeling-oriented love is largely, if not entirely, self-seeking. Plus, feelings are fleeting and hard to control, not to mention limiting. It's impossible to love everyone in the secular sense because it's impossible to have positive feelings toward everyone, but it is possible to love everyone in the Christian sense because it's possible to wish everyone good.

But again, we must be careful. Christian love is not only good thoughts or intentions. It doesn't just think (or hit the Like button on Facebook). It acts. Christian love is a verb. It is something you do. It is service to others. Jean Lasserre elaborates:

> What does it mean to love your neighbour? Jesus has explicitly replied to this question in the parable of the Good Samaritan. To love my neighbour is to come to his aid, to give him what he may have need of, to forgive him for what he is and what he has done; it is to put myself at his service (John 13:15; Gal. 5:13). It is to be

really there for him, to bear his burdens (Gal. 6:2), to respect his calling and help him to realize it. In a word, it is to give myself to him, as Jesus gave Himself to me. But it is not a matter of sentiment; it is a concrete attitude which expresses itself in acts.[29]

James states it more bluntly: "Suppose a brother or a sister is without clothes and daily food. If one of you says to them, 'Go in peace; keep warm and well fed,' but does nothing about their physical needs, what good is it?" (James 2:15-16). Likewise, the author of 1 John asks, "If anyone has material possessions and sees a brother or sister in need but has no pity on them, how can the love of God be in that person?" (1 John 3:17). Therefore, he continues, "let us not love with words or speech but with actions and in truth" (v. 18).

Christian love is so much more than secular love—and so much more beautiful. It is, in Wynkoop's words, "the correction of man's limited, selfish, selective, perverted love."[30]

Christian Love vs. Violence

Hopefully the chasm between Christian love and violence is already coming into view. Christian love is wholly nonviolent. None of the characteristics of love we just reviewed involve or endorse the use of any violence. Try to imagine being violently patient, violently forgiving, or violently selfless toward someone. Try to picture yourself violently practicing hospitality, violently blessing those who persecute you, or violently repaying evil with good. Have you ever been violently gentle, violently kind, or violently generous? Me neither.

On the other hand, the vices God has commanded us to avoid (e.g., greed, envy, wrath, pride, thievery, drunkenness, slander, jealousy, and selfish ambition) are all either violent themselves or frequently lead to violence. Have you ever been so envious, so angry, or so offended that you wanted to or did resort to violence? Me too. Here's how James described the problem: "What causes fights and quarrels among you? Don't they come from your desires that battle within you? You desire but do not have, so you kill. You covet but you cannot get what you want, so you quarrel and fight" (James 4:1-2). The first act of violence in the Bible, Cain's murder of Abel, proves the point. It was the product of jealousy.[31]

The biblical command to love orders us to adopt wholly nonviolent traits and avoid those that are vulnerable to violence.

Furthermore, the Golden Rule leaves no room for violence. We don't want others using violence against us so we shouldn't use it against them.[32] The same goes for the command to love others as we love ourselves (since we don't use violence against ourselves, unless we are psychologically impaired) and the command to love our enemies (for if we are not to use violence against our enemies then against whom can we use it?). And, as the next few chapters will demonstrate, Jesus's example also excludes all violence, because he never used it.

In short, everything the Bible says about love—how it is defined, described, and exemplified—testifies to its complete nonviolence.

Of course, Christian love isn't merely nonviolence. It doesn't simply refrain from using violence against others. It goes beyond nonviolence to proactively and self-sacrificially serve others. Christian love isn't only the absence of violence; it is the presence of good deeds.

The biblical version of the Golden Rule bears this out. It is uniquely proactive. In contrast to all other pre-Jesus versions, it requires not that we simply *refrain* from doing to others what we don't want done to us but that we *do* to others what we want done to us.[33] As Donald Kraybill notes, "Jesus flipped the negative rule upside down and turned it into a directive for action."[34]

Here's another way to look at it: not only is Christian love nonviolent, it is the opposite of violent. Whereas violence harms, destroys, and tears down, Christian love serves, restores, and builds up. Take another look at the love-defining characteristics listed earlier (e.g., gentleness, forgiveness, patience, self-control, kindness, selflessness, etc.) and try to describe the opposite of violence better than they do. It's difficult, if not impossible.

Christian love opposes violence. It isn't indifferent to violence. It is antagonistic to it. Christian love is antiviolence. It doesn't just refrain from violence. It attacks and overcomes it. It just does so nonviolently, through self-sacrificial acts of service.

This is why terms like nonresistance and nonretaliation don't do justice to the notion of Christian pacifism. Christian pacifism isn't passive. It isn't about sitting idly by, refusing to resist or retaliate. It absolutely resists and retaliates. It just does so nonviolently. It's a refusal to use violence, not a refusal to do anything. Christian pacifism is active, nonviolent peacemaking. It is not "nonresistance" but "nonviolent resistance." It is *pacif*ism, not *passiv*ism.

In conclusion, Christian love is much more than nonviolence, but nonviolence is the essential first step. To paraphrase Paul, love first does no harm.[35] This makes sense. The first way we serve others is to refrain from harming them. As such, nonviolence is the foundation of Christian ethics. It is the bedrock upon which all other good deeds are built. Thus, Christian love *requires* nonviolence.

Now that we've got a broad understanding of the heart and soul of Christian ethics, love, let's take a look at Jesus's other teachings.

---

[1] Throughout this book, I use masculine pronouns and analogies for God not because I think he is male, or even that he has a gender, but because that is what the Bible most often—though not always—does.

[2] See also Mark 12:28-34.

[3] By the way, the two greatest commandments never conflict. Loving others never takes the form of acting unlovingly toward God. And loving God never takes the form of acting unlovingly toward others. Loving others is central to what it means to love God. As the author of 1 John explains, "Whoever claims to love God yet hates a brother or sister is a liar. For whoever does not love their brother and sister, whom they have seen, cannot love God, whom they have not seen. And he has given us this command: Anyone who loves God must also love their brother and sister" (1 John 4:20-21). To love others is to express our love for God.

[4] Matt. 7:12; 22:40.

[5] See also Gal. 5:14 and James 2:8.

[6] Rom. 13:8.

[7] Mildred Bangs Wynkoop, *A Theology of Love: The Dynamic of Wesleyanism* 2nd Edition (Beacon Hill Press of Kansas City, 2015), 468, Kindle.

[8] 1 John 3:14-15; 4:7, 8, 10, 12, 16; Luke 10:25-28; James 2:5; John 3:16.

[9] 1 Cor. 13:13.

[10] Wynkoop, *A Theology of Love*, 4157.

[11] 1 Cor. 13:1-3.

[12] 1 Cor. 13:8; 1 Pet. 4:8.

[13] John 13:35; 1 John 3:10.

[14] 1 John 3:11; 2 John 1:5; Deut. 6:4-9; Lev. 19:18.

[15] Although this is the Bible's most comprehensive definition of love, it isn't necessarily complete. Paul doesn't intend it to be. He isn't trying to abstractly define biblical love here. He is highlighting the aspects of biblical love that he believes the Corinthian church needs to hear.

[16] See 1 Cor. 13:4-7. These attributes are repeated throughout the New Testament. For a few more examples, see 1 Thess. 3:12; 4:7, 11; 5:14, 15, 22; 2 Thess. 3:12; Rom. 12:9, 13, 14, 18, 19, 21; 14:19; James 1:19; 4:10; 5:10; 1 Pet. 1:15; 2:20-21; 3:11, 17; 4:1, 16; 5:5; 2 Pet. 1:6; Titus 1:8; 3:1-2, 8; Eph. 2:10; 4:2; Gal. 5:22-23; Col. 1:11; 3:13; 1 Tim. 2:2; 2 Tim. 2:3, 4:5.

[17] Rom. 12:9-21

[18] Exod. 20:1-17; Deut. 5:4-21; Rom. 13:9-10.

[19] 1 Cor. 13:13; Gal. 5:22-23; 2 Pet. 1:5-7; Col. 3:12-13.

[20] Prov. 6:16-19; 1 Cor. 6:9-11; Gal. 5:19-21; Eph. 5:5.

[21] Matt. 7:12; 22:39; Mark 12:31; Gal. 5:14; James 2:8; Rom. 13:9.

[22] See also Matt. 7:12.

[23] For commands to love like Jesus loved, see John 13:15, 34; 14:12; 15:12; 1 Cor. 3:11; 11:1; 1 Pet. 2:21; Phil. 2:5; 1 John 2:6; 3:16; 4:9-11; Col 2:6; 3:17; Eph. 5:1-2; Matt. 20:26-28; and Mark 10:43-45. For commands to love as Jesus taught us to love, see Matt. 7:5, 24; 17:1-5; 28:18-20; Luke 6:46-48; John 14:15, 21, 23-24; 15:14; Acts 3:22; 1 Cor. 9:20-21; Gal. 2:15-16; 3:23-25; and 2 Thess. 1:8.

[24] Rom. 5:8; 1 John 4:10-11, 19; Eph. 2:1-5.

[25] Matt. 5:44-48; Luke 6:27-36; Ps. 136:26; Rom. 8:38-39.

[26] Matt. 5:43-48; Luke 6:27-36; 10:25-37; Rom. 12:14-21.

[27] C. S. Lewis, *Mere Christianity* (New York, NY: HarperOne, 2001), 132.

[28] Martin Luther King, Jr., *A Gift of Love: Sermons from Strength to Love and Other Preachings* (Beacon Press, 2012), 773, Kindle.

[29] Jean Lasserre, *War and the Gospel*, trans. Oliver Coburn (Eugene, OR: Wipf & Stock, 1998), 24.

[30] Wynkoop, *A Theology of Love*, 246.

[31] Gen. 4.

[32] It's impossible to want others to use violence against you because violence is by definition unwanted. If you *want* someone to use physical force against you, it isn't violence. It's just physical force.

[33] Matt. 7:12; Luke 6:31.

[34] Donald B. Kraybill, *The Upside-Down Kingdom* Updated Edition (Herald Press, 2012), 2787, Kindle.

[35] Rom. 13:10.

CHAPTER 2

JESUS'S OTHER TEACHINGS

In this chapter, we will analyze Jesus's other commands, the Sermon on the Mount, how Jesus responded to his followers' violence, and how he sent his disciples into the world. As you'll discover, each sends a clear and consistent antiviolence message.

Commands

Although moral principles can be deduced from almost everything Jesus said, and although he issued many commands that obviously don't apply to us today (like the context-specific command to fetch him a donkey to ride), Jesus dispensed only about fifty timeless, universally applicable, explicit commands. Of those fifty, slightly less than half apply to how we interact with others, as opposed to how we interact with God. With the caveat that compiling a condensed list of Jesus's commands is a bit of an art form and lends itself to minor, reasonable variations,[1] here is a complete list of Jesus's commands regarding how we are to treat others:

- Resolve disputes quickly and directly before others get involved. (Matt. 5:25; 18:15-17)
- Forgive all others' offenses against you. (Matt. 18:21-22; Mark 11:25-26)
- Do not respond to evil with evil, but turn the other cheek. (Matt. 5:38-39)
- Give more than is asked or required of you. (Matt. 5:40–42)
- Don't covet or be greedy. (Luke 12:15)
- Don't steal. (Mark 10:19; Luke 18:20)
- Keep your word/promises. (Matt. 5:37)
- Don't give false testimony. (Mark 10:19; Luke 18:20)
- Be merciful. (Luke 6:36)
- Don't judge others. (Matt. 7:1-2)
- While in the world, be as wise as snakes and as innocent as doves. (Matt. 10:16)

- Don't despise children. (Matt. 18:10)
- Honor marriage and don't commit adultery. (Matt. 19:6; 5:27-28)
- Honor your parents. (Matt. 15:4)
- Give to Caesar what is his. (Matt. 22:19-21)
- Don't murder. (Mark 10:19; Luke 18:20)
- Love others as you love yourself and as Jesus loves you. (Matt. 22:39; Mark 12:28-31; Luke 10:25-28; John 13:34; 15:12)
- Treat others how you want to be treated. (Matt. 7:12; Luke 6:31)
- Love and pray for your enemies. (Matt. 5:44; Luke 6:35)
- Be a humble servant to others. (Matt. 20:26-28; 23:11-12; John 13:14-15)
- Feed, clothe, shelter, and care for others. (John 21:15-16; Matt. 25:34-36; Luke 10:30-37)
- Extend hospitality to the poor. (Luke 14:12-14)
- Allow others to see your good deeds. (Matt. 5:15-16)
- Make disciples of others and baptize them. (Matt. 28:19)
- Teach others to obey my commandments. (Matt. 28:20)

Of course, all of these are paraphrases of what Jesus actually said and none are presented in context, so some may not mean exactly what a surface reading suggests. Nonetheless, even such a crude list tells us a few important things about Jesus's view of violence.

Jesus hasn't commanded a single act of violence. None of his commands instruct us to use any violence against any other person for any reason. Not one. Not even for the purpose of enforcing human justice. Assuming he has commanded us to do everything he wants us to do, which seems reasonable, his commands give violence *no* role.

Not only are Jesus's commands entirely nonviolent, many are *anti*violence. A few command us to refrain from specific types of violence, like theft and murder. Others instruct us to refrain from behaviors and thoughts that often lead to violence—don't respond to evil with evil, don't commit adultery, don't bear false witness, don't covet, don't judge, etc. And still others demand we do things that prevent or diffuse violence—resolve disputes quickly, forgive, be merciful, keep our promises, humbly serve others, etc.

All of Jesus's commands align with what we learned about Christian love in the previous chapter: it is both wholly nonviolent and always antiviolence. This makes sense. Jesus's overarching command regarding how to treat others, the one that summarizes all of his other commands, is to love them.

Therefore, while it's true that Jesus didn't explicitly command us to never use any violence, it is implied by what he did and didn't command.

Sermon on the Mount

The Sermon on the Mount is Jesus's most well-known sermon and the longest, most thorough, most important explanation of how to embody God's kingdom on earth (i.e., how to do his will).[2] According to John R. W. Stott, "It is the nearest thing to a manifesto that he [Jesus] ever uttered, for it is his own description of what he wanted his followers to be and to do."[3] Saint Augustine referred to it as the "perfect standard of the Christian life."[4] John Howard Yoder[5] called it "the most concentrated statement of the ethical demand of Jesus."[6] Richard Hays declared it the "definitive charter for the life of the new covenant community."[7] J. Denny Weaver believes it "spells out ... what it means to live out the reign of God."[8] D. Stephen Long asserts its "beatitudes are the forms of life that are necessary for us to live as citizens of God's coming Kingdom, the one we pray for every day in the Lord's Prayer."[9] Robin R. Meyers claims "few would argue with the assertion that the Sermon on the Mount is the Constitution of the Christian faith."[10]

To be sure, the Sermon on the Mount is nothing less than the fundamental blueprint for how to live a distinctly Christian life. It is also arguably the most important speech ever given—on any topic. And, most importantly for our purposes, it is entirely antiviolence, containing no pro-violence statements and many antiviolence ones. In fact, Christians and non-Christians alike consider it *the* speech on nonviolence. Let's look at its most violence-related parts.

Jesus began the sermon by listing the characteristics of those who embody God's kingdom, a list we call the Beatitudes:

Blessed are the poor in spirit,
    for theirs is the kingdom of heaven.

Blessed are those who mourn,

for they will be comforted.

Blessed are the meek,
  for they will inherit the earth.

Blessed are those who hunger and thirst for righteousness,
  for they will be filled.

Blessed are the merciful,
  for they will be shown mercy.

Blessed are the pure in heart,
  for they will see God.

Blessed are the peacemakers,
  for they will be called children of God.

Blessed are those who are persecuted because of righteousness,
  for theirs is the kingdom of heaven.

Blessed are you when people insult you, persecute you and falsely
say all kinds of evil against you because of me. (Matt. 5:3-11)

From the start, Jesus expresses a clear preference for nonviolent characteristics. Every one of those attributes is incompatible with using violence. He does not praise the powerful, the rulers of history, or the enforcers of justice. It is the humble, gentle, peaceful, submissive, sympathetic, forgiving, righteous, and persecuted who inhabit his kingdom, not those who wield force on his behalf. As professor Thomas Trzyna notes, the Beatitudes "present in a compressed form a philosophy of life that is consistent only with a pacifist position."[11]

A few statements later, Jesus indicated he wants us to be so nonviolent that we don't even think violent thoughts when he broadened the command against murder to prohibit mere anger as well: "You have heard that it was said ... 'You shall not murder, and anyone who murders will be subject to judgment.' But I tell you that anyone who is angry with a brother or sister will be subject to judgment" (Matt. 5:21-22). Violent acts like murder are so evil, says Jesus, we shouldn't even entertain the thoughts that lead to them.

Jesus scattered similar exhortations throughout the sermon. He commands us to store up treasure in heaven instead of on earth, "where thieves break in and steal" (Matt. 6:19). How often do humans resort to violence to acquire or defend earthly treasure? He commands us to not worry about what we will eat, drink, or wear.[12] How often does our worry about such things lead to violence? He commands us to not judge, "For in the same way you judge others, you will be judged, and with the measure you use, it will be measured to you" (Matt. 7:2). How often does our tendency toward judgment produce overzealous violent retribution, retribution that perpetuates the cycle of violence?

Soon after condemning violence-inducing thoughts, Jesus issued one of his most famous, and most controversial, antiviolence commands:

> You have heard that it was said, "Eye for eye, and tooth for tooth." But I tell you, do not resist an evil person. If anyone slaps you on the right cheek, turn to them the other cheek also. And if anyone wants to sue you and take your shirt, hand over your coat as well. If anyone forces you to go one mile, go with them two miles. Give to the one who asks you, and do not turn away from the one who wants to borrow from you. (Matt. 5:38-42)[13]

The first thing we need to understand about this passage is that Jesus is prohibiting *violent* resistance to evil, not all types of resistance to evil. The phrase often rendered as "do not resist" is more accurately understood as "do not *violently* resist." N.T. Wright's translation makes this explicit: "But I say to you: don't use violence to resist evil!" Wink elaborates:

> When the court translators working in the hire of King James chose to translate *antistēnai* as "Resist not evil," they were doing something more than rendering Greek into English. They were translating nonviolent resistance into docility. Jesus did not tell his oppressed hearers not to resist evil. That would have been absurd. His entire ministry is utterly at odds with such a preposterous idea. The Greek word is made up of two parts: anti, a word still used in English for "against," and *histēmi*, a verb that in its noun form (stasis) means violent rebellion, armed revolt, sharp dissention...
>
> A proper translation of Jesus's teaching would then be, "Don't strike back at evil (or, one who has done you evil) in kind." "Do not retaliate against violence with violence." The Scholars Version is brilliant: "Don't react violently against the one who is evil." Jesus was no less committed to opposing evil than the anti-Roman resistance fighters. The only difference was over the means to be used: how one should fight evil.[14]

It doesn't get much more nonviolent than to command others to not even use violence against evil. What's left to use violence against?

Next, notice that Jesus labeled three relatively minor acts of violence "evil." After commanding his audience to refrain from violently resisting evil, he provided three examples of evil acts that shouldn't be resisted: a hit on the cheek, a wrongful lawsuit, and twenty minutes of forced labor. Those examples imply that even the slightest violence, even violence that is merely insulting or temporarily inconveniencing, is evil.

We've already discussed the two remaining violence-related instructions in the Sermon on the Mount in the previous chapter: the command to love our enemies and the command to follow the Golden Rule.[15] To reiterate, both of them prohibit all violence, since (1) if we are not to use violence against even our enemies, then against whom can we use it? and (2) we don't want others using violence against us, so we shouldn't use it against them.

That's the Sermon on the Mount's antiviolence message in a nutshell. It's unambiguous. It's the most complete picture Jesus gave of what it looks like to embody God's kingdom on earth and it highlights nonviolence as a *primary* component.

Unfortunately, although almost everyone agrees that the Sermon on the Mount is thoroughly antiviolence, many Christians believe its radical demands don't apply to them. Fallen humans have concocted a plethora of excuses over the years for sidestepping its call:

- Jesus directed it at his twelve disciples and only ever meant it for them.
- It is a special standard of conduct that only applies to the holiest among us, like priests, monks, and saints, not to normal, everyday Christians.
- It applies to our inward dispositions, our thoughts and attitudes, not our everyday public lives.
- It applied during the simple time of first century Palestine, but not in today's much more complex world.
- It applies to Christians who don't have access to power, but not those who do.
- It is too impractical, too ineffective.

- Because it's impossible to achieve, it is merely an ideal we are called to pray and hope for, not try to embody.
- Jesus was trying to show us how sinful and in need of God's grace we are, not how to live.
- God doesn't want us interpreting it legalistically, so it surely can't mean what it says.

The list goes on. Ultimately, however, all of our excuses, all of our attempts to water down the sermon's antiviolence and explain it away, fail.

For starters, Jesus wasn't speaking in private or only to his disciples. The sermon opens with: "Now when Jesus saw *the crowds*, he went up on a mountainside and sat down" (Matt. 5:1). And it closes with: "When Jesus had finished saying these things, *the crowds* were amazed at his teaching, because he taught as one who had authority, and not as their teachers of the law" (Matt. 7:28-29). Clearly, the venue indicates Jesus's audience was all of his followers, then and now.

In fact, in the sermon itself, Jesus explicitly and repeatedly proclaimed that it applied to everyone. "Therefore *anyone* who sets aside one of the least of these commands and teaches others accordingly will be called least in the kingdom of heaven, but *whoever* practices and teaches these commands will be called great in the kingdom of heaven" (Matt. 5:19). "So in *everything*, do to others what you would have them do to you, for this sums up the Law and the Prophets" (Matt. 7:12). "Not everyone who says to me, 'Lord, Lord,' will enter the kingdom of heaven, but only *the one who does* the will of my Father who is in heaven"—the will he had just described (Matt. 7:21). As Dallas Willard observed, "almost one sixth of the entire Discourse (fifteen of ninety-two verses) is devoted to emphasizing the importance of actually doing what it says."[16]

Jesus even ended the sermon with a final, unambiguous, emphatic plea for everyone to obey everything he had just taught:

> Therefore everyone who hears these words of mine and puts them into practice is like a wise man who built his house on the rock. The rain came down, the streams rose, and the winds blew and beat against that house; yet it did not fall, because it had its foundation on the rock. But everyone who hears these words of mine and does not put them into practice is like a foolish man who

built his house on sand. The rain came down, the streams rose, and the winds blew and beat against that house, and it fell with a great crash. (Matt. 7:24-27)

Could Jesus have been more straightforward? Does this sound like someone who wants his listeners to partially disregard his instructions?[17] Does it sound like Jesus is primarily concerned about what we believe, instead of how we act? Or like he is merely describing what life will be like after we die, instead of how we should live today?

In addition, the sermon is full of practical instructions on how to implement many of its directives, which obviously suggests Jesus intended them to be implemented. Stanley Hauerwas and William H. Willimon explain:

> It is here that we often say things like, "Well, Jesus was speaking for himself. He was the best person who has ever lived. He never intended for us to follow this way literally." Yet what impresses about the Sermon is its attention to the nitty-gritty details of everyday life. Jesus appears to be giving very practical, very explicit directions for what to do when someone has done you wrong, when someone attacks you, when you are married to someone. It is clear that Jesus certainly *thought* he was giving us practical, everyday guidance on how to live like disciples.[18]

The Sermon on the Mount is not wishful thinking. Jesus didn't provide such instructions so we could deem them too impractical and then disregard them as inapplicable to the reality of our fallen world.

As we will see throughout this book, everything Jesus said and did confirms that he intended for everyone to obey the sermon. He exemplified all of its instructions, even in how he died, and encouraged others to do the same. In the Great Commission, for example, he told his disciples to "go and make disciples of all nations … teaching them to obey *everything* I have commanded you" (Matt. 28:19-20). Everything obviously includes his most important sermon. At least the disciples thought so, as they devoted their lives to obeying and preaching Jesus's instructions. In reality, it's impossible to claim the sermon wasn't meant to be obeyed but everything else Jesus and the apostles taught was because they all teach the same things, just in varying degrees of explicitness.

Nothing in the sermon itself or anywhere else in the New Testament limits its instructions to the particularly devout or to those who feel a special calling toward pacifism. Instead, everything indicates that they apply to the everyday actions of everyone who desires to follow Jesus. "Jesus is not talking about the difference between pacifists and other Christians," writes Yoder. "Jesus is talking about the difference between people who listen to him and those who do not."[19]

When we read the entire sermon carefully and in context, we realize all of our other excuses for not obeying Jesus fail as well. Here are two quick examples:

First, the sermon is not merely about inward thoughts and feelings, but about outward behavior too. Jesus wasn't saying, "As long as your inward disposition toward someone who strikes you on the cheek is loving, you can respond by breaking his nose." He wasn't telling us we can transform impermissible violent behavior into permissible violent behavior by first cultivating the right internal thoughts and feelings—or that we can act hatefully toward our enemies as long as we internally love them, as if such an incompatible state is possible. Jesus wasn't explaining how to ensure the violence we commit is holy and pleasing to God. He was teaching us that violence is incompatible with the kingdom of God, so incompatible that we shouldn't even think the thoughts that produce it.

Second, the sermon isn't only about private behavior. It's also about public behavior. When Jesus replaced "eye for an eye" with "do not resist an evil person," he was replacing one of Israel's core legal principles. He was speaking about how to respond to *social* evils, like when someone sues you in a court of law or when government conscripts your labor.

The excuses we recite, in order to avoid simple, literal obedience to Jesus's clear instructions in the Sermon on the Mount, are not scripturally based. They are imposed on the text by our fallen desire to go our own way.

Most importantly for our purposes, the Sermon on the Mount's commands, which apply to everyone who wants to follow Jesus today, are wholly nonviolent from start to finish. That being said, however, the Christian case for nonviolence doesn't hinge on any particular interpretation of the Sermon on the Mount. As we have already seen and will continue to see throughout this book, it is much more extensive than that.

Jesus's Fulfillment of the Law

There's one more antiviolence aspect of the Sermon on the Mount worth mentioning: Jesus's fulfillment of the law.[20] Near the start of the sermon, he proclaimed that he had come to "fulfill" the law (not abolish it) and then he repeatedly declared, "You have heard it said … but I tell you …" (Matt. 5:17-45). What Jesus meant by "fulfill" is key.

Recall that the Bible is a narrative, not an encyclopedia or constitution. As such, it reveals God's will within an ongoing, developing story, not in standalone rules meted out one verse, paragraph, or incident at a time. This is particularly true for God's ethical revelation. He didn't fly by earth one day and drop off a finalized list of universally and eternally applicable moral rules. Instead, through Israel, God first met humans where they were at, established a relationship with them, instituted initial improvements, and generally laid the groundwork for his ethical ideal, which he later revealed in Jesus.

So, when Jesus said he came to "fulfill" the law, he did not mean that he came to discard it or render it obsolete. He did not mean that he came to meet its requirements or to satisfy its demands so we no longer have to, or that he came to appease God's need for perfect obedience, thereby releasing us from the need to obey. Fulfillment in those senses would have been abolishment, which Jesus rejected.

Instead, Jesus meant that he came to finish what God had started in the Old Testament. He came to finalize his ethical revelation—to complete it, to bring it into full bloom. He came to provide us with God's perfect, eternal, and universally applicable moral code. He came to reveal God's ethical ideal, to show us exactly what God wants from every human. Instead of coming to excuse us from obedience, he came to show us how to perfectly obey.

This is what Jesus was doing in the Sermon on the Mount, particularly in the six antitheses. He was revealing God's ethical ideal by taking fundamental components of the Old Testament law and expanding them to their moral conclusions.[21] For example, he took the prohibition against murder and expanded it into a prohibition against anger and a call for reconciliation;[22] he took the command against adultery and expanded it into a command against even lust;[23] he took the limited retaliation of an "eye for an eye" (which was a moral advancement in its time) and expanded it into complete non-retaliation by commanding us to turn the other cheek;[24] and he took the notion of loving your neighbor and expanded it into loving everyone, even your enemy.[25]

Notice the antiviolence theme running through the heart of Jesus's fulfillment of the law. He always directed the law toward less violence. In fact, he removed all remaining violence from the law, thereby completing the pacifying process God began in the Old Testament.[26] In addition to the examples cited in the previous paragraph, recall that Jesus eventually summarized his entire fulfillment of the law in the command to *love* God and others, with love being defined as not only nonviolence but also antiviolence.[27]

We must not lose sight of the legal and theological context in which Jesus made his radical antiviolence statements. He inherited a set of laws and traditions that endorsed the restrained, just use of violence. He could have embraced such precedent. Like the Old Testament Israelites, Jesus could have employed limited violence and justified it by referencing God's Old Testament laws. But he didn't. Instead, he overturned the Old Testament's violence in every regard. Jesus "fulfilled" the law by rewriting it to exclude all violence, and in the process, he pacified Christian ethics.

How Jesus Responded to His Followers' Violence

When one of Jesus's disciples, Peter, attempted to prevent Jesus's arrest by drawing his sword and cutting off a man's ear, Jesus rebuked him and said, "Put your sword back in its place" (Matt. 26:52). Then he made three important points about the use of violence. First, he issued a general, practical warning against its use, saying, "all who draw the sword will die by the sword" (Matt. 26:52). Then he chastised Peter for thinking he needed his violent help, asking him, "Do you think I cannot call on my Father, and he will at once put at my disposal more than twelve legions of angels?" (Matt. 26:53). Lastly, he chided the crowd that had brought violent weapons to arrest him, asking them, "Am I leading a rebellion that you have come out with swords and clubs to capture me? Every day I sat in the temple courts teaching, and you did not arrest me" (Matt. 26:55).

In other words, when one of Jesus's followers attempted to use what many would consider justified, defensive violence, Jesus scolded him, issued a general condemnation of violence, stated he had the ability to employ vast amounts of violence but chose not to, and pointed out how ridiculous it was to view him as a violent rebel.

From what we know of the rest of Peter's life, he took Jesus's rebuke seriously. The Bible never depicts him using violence again. He put his sword back in its place, left it there, and encouraged others to do the same, instructing them to follow Jesus's example of nonretaliation and voluntary suffering.[28]

In a similar incident, when two of Jesus's disciples, James and John, asked Jesus if he wanted them to "call fire down from heaven to destroy" a group of Samaritan villagers who had refused to welcome him, Jesus rebuked them and went to a different village (Luke 9:51-56). Some Bible translations, like the New King James Version, indicate that Jesus also added, "You do not know what manner of spirit you are of. For the Son of Man did not come to destroy men's lives but to save them." Regardless of whether Jesus explicitly attributed the origin of their desire to use violence to Satan instead of God, his rebuke implicitly sent the same message.

These are the only two instances in the New Testament in which Jesus's followers used or advocated using violence in his presence, and in both cases Jesus swiftly and definitively denounced such violence, even when it was a simple attempt to protect him against unjust arrest, torture, and murder. No wonder Jesus told a Roman governor that his true followers do not use violence.[29] More on that encounter later.

How Jesus Sent His Disciples Into the World

When Jesus sent his disciples into the world, he told them he was sending them out "like sheep among wolves" (Matt. 10:16). He didn't send them out as wolves among wolves. He sent them out as non-predators among predators. Sheep are some of the least violent, most docile animals on earth. They are physically vulnerable and harmless. They are, in short, the animal equivalent of pacifists.

After the sheep comparison, Jesus added, "Therefore be as shrewd as snakes and as innocent as doves." Not hawks. Not eagles. Not even pigeons. Doves. Fragile, little, gentle, peaceful doves.

When Jesus gave his final instructions to his disciples in the Great Commission, he commanded them to make disciples of all nations by "baptizing them in the name of the Father and of the Son and of the Holy Spirit, and teaching them to obey everything I have commanded you" (Matt. 28:19-20). Baptizing and teaching. That's how Jesus wants us to advance God's kingdom on earth.

Similarly, when Jesus's disciples asked him who among them would be given the most power and prestige in his kingdom, he condemned their desire and commanded them to serve others instead of "lord" over them. Here's his entire response:

> You know that the rulers of the Gentiles lord it over them, and their high officials exercise authority over them. Not so with you. Instead, whoever wants to become great among you must be your servant, and whoever wants to be first must be your slave—just as the Son of Man did not come to be served, but to serve, and to give his life as a ransom for many. (Matt. 20:25-28)[30]

As I'll explain in more detail in Chapter 8, Jesus wants us to advance his kingdom by speaking and embodying the truth, not by resorting to violence or politics or any other human power. Instead of seeking to rule, he instructs us to become servants, and instead of trying to control others, he commands us to simply love them.

Our moral mandate is entirely nonviolent.

Except for Jesus's violent parables, which we will examine in Chapter 5, that's all of his most violence-related teachings. Now let's look at a few passages that are often misinterpreted as not only discussing the ethics of violence but as promoting violence.

---

[1] Some compilers have come up with over 100, such as J.S. McConnell's 147 located at www.wowzone.com/commandm.htm and Peter Wittstock's book *Hear Him! The One Hundred Twenty-Five Commands of Jesus*. I've presented the shorter, more consolidated list of fifty to avoid the duplication that seems prevalent in such longer lists. However, even the condensed lists of about fifty commands contain variations. For two examples, see Bill McGinnis' "Complete List of the Commands of Christ" at http://patriot.net/~bmcgin/pearl-thecommandmentsofjesus.html and Matthew Robert Payne's article "The Fifty Commands of Jesus" at http://ezinearticles.com/?The-Fifty-Commands-of-Jesus&id=468177.

[2] Matt. 5-7.

[3] Michael Babcock, *Unchristian America: Living With Faith in a Nation That Was Never Under God* (SaltRiver, 2008), 193.

4 Augustine, *The Quotable Augustine*, ed. Phillip H. Melton (Washington, D.C.: The Catholic University of America Press, 2016), 12.

5 Despite Yoder's sordid history of sexual assault, which I wholeheartedly condemn, I quote him throughout my writing for a few reasons. First, he isn't just another Christian pacifist. He is a (if not *the*) towering intellectual figure in nonviolence theology and his work has deeply influenced my own. Therefore, I feel it deserves attribution. Second, I've erred on the side of grace. Given my need for it, granting it to Yoder only seems wise. Other than Jesus, no one quoted in this book was perfect. You'll even find a quote or two from the serial adulterer Martin Luther King, Jr. Consequently, singling out Yoder for special exclusion and shaming strikes me as hypocritical on multiple levels. Third, I don't quote Yoder to justify sexual assault. On the contrary, I quote only his staunch antiviolence views. Granted, doing so involves a bit of irony, but such irony is present anytime a fellow sinner is quoted. No fallen human has ever perfectly lived up to the theology he has espoused. At the end of the day, I've chosen to adopt the stance of institutions like the Anabaptist Mennonite Biblical Seminary (at which Yoder taught at the time of the abuse) and theologians like Stanley Hauerwas, Marva J. Dawn, Ronald J. Sider, J. Denny Weaver, Gayle Gerber Koontz, and Mark Thiessen Nation, all of whom deeply regret and condemn Yoder's sins but continue to study and disseminate his important antiviolence (and therefore implicitly anti-sexual abuse) theology.

6 John Howard Yoder, *The Original Revolution: Essays on Christian Pacifism*, Revised Edition (Herald Press, 2012), 1142, Kindle.

7 Richard Hays, *The Moral Vision of the New Testament: Community, Cross, New Creation; A Contemporary Introduction to New Testament Ethic* (HarperOne, 2013), 8991, Kindle.

8 J. Denny Weaver, *God Without Violence: Following a Nonviolent God in a Violent World* (Cascade Books, 2016), 957, Kindle.

9 D. Stephen Long, *A Faith Not Worth Fighting For: Addressing Commonly Asked Questions about Christian Nonviolence* (The Peaceable Kingdom Series), ed. Tripp York and Justin Bronson Barringer (Cascade Books, 2012), 512, Kindle.

10 Robin R. Meyers, *Saving Jesus from the Church: How to Stop Worshipping Christ and Start Following Jesus* (HarperCollins, 2009), 2959, Kindle.

11 Thomas Trzyna, *Blessed Are the Pacifists: The Beatitudes and Just War Theory* (Herald Press, 2006), 35, Kindle.

12 Matt. 6:25-34.

13 See also Luke 6:27-31.

14 Walter Wink, *Christian Peace and Nonviolence: A Documentary History*, ed. Michael G. Long (Maryknoll, NY: Orbis Books, 2011) 9. For two more

excellent explanations of why Matthew 5:39 should be translated as "do not *violently* resist evil," see (1) page 34 in Ronald J. Sider's *If Jesus is Lord: Loving Our Enemies in an Age of Violence*, Kindle Edition (Baker Academic, 2019) and (2) page 214 in John Dominic Crossan's *How to Read the Bible and Still Be a Christian: Struggling with Divine Violence from Genesis Through Revelation*, Kindle Edition (HarperCollins, 2015).

[15] Matt. 5:43-48; 7:12.

[16] Dallas Willard, *The Divine Conspiracy: Rediscovering Our Hidden Life in God* (HarperCollins, 2009), 2641, Kindle.

[17] If your mother, your boss, or a government bureaucrat said these same things to you, would you take them seriously? Would you obey? You would. So why not also your Lord and Savior?

[18] Stanley Hauerwas and William H. Willimon, *Resident Aliens: Life in the Christian Colony* Expanded 25th Anniversary Edition (Abingdon Press, 2014), 2634, Kindle.

[19] John Howard Yoder, *He Came Preaching Peace* (Eugene, OR: Wipf & Stock, 1998), 47.

[20] I discuss this concept at length in my book *The Old Testament Case for Nonviolence*, including how we know God used incremental ethical revelation, why he used it, how we know Jesus finalized it, and what his finalization means for our use of violence. See Chapters 2-5.

[21] Remember, by making these changes, Jesus wasn't transgressing the Old Testament law. He was transcending it. He wasn't abolishing it. He was elevating it. He wasn't diminishing it. He was bringing it to its fullest expression.

[22] Matt. 5:21-24.

[23] Matt. 5:27-28.

[24] Matt. 5:38-42.

[25] Matt. 5:43-48.

[26] For a discussion of how God's commands to Old Testament Israel, although barbaric by our current standards, were an ethical improvement by the ancient world's standards, see Chapter 2 in *The Old Testament Case for Nonviolence*.

[27] Matt. 22:35-40.

[28] 1 Pet. 2:21-23.

[29] John 18:36.

[30] See also Mark 10:35-45, Luke 22:24-30, and 1 Pet. 5:1-4.

CHAPTER 3

COMMONLY MISINTERPRETED TEACHINGS

In this chapter, we will analyze Jesus's statement about bringing not peace but a sword, his command to buy swords, and his complimentary encounter with a centurion. As you'll see, these events don't even address the ethics of violence, let alone promote its use.

I Came to Bring a Sword

In Matthew 10:34, Jesus said, "Do not suppose that I have come to bring peace to earth. I did not come to bring peace, but a sword." Non-pacifists often cite this statement to justify the use of violence, but for numerous reasons, it doesn't. To see why, we simply need to review its biblical context—immediate, intermediate, and broad.

The immediate context below indicates that Jesus was speaking figuratively about the division he and his message would cause, rather than literally about a sword.

> Do not suppose that I have come to bring peace to the earth. I did not come to bring peace, but a sword. For I have come to turn "a man against his father, a daughter against her mother, a daughter-in-law against her mother-in-law—a man's enemies will be the members of his own household." Anyone who loves their father or mother more than me is not worthy of me; anyone who loves their son or daughter more than me is not worthy of me. Whoever does not take up their cross and follow me is not worthy of me. Whoever finds their life will lose it, and whoever loses their life for my sake will find it. (Matt. 10:34-39)

Luke's account makes the figurative nature of the metaphor even clearer by using the word *division* instead of *sword*: "Do you think I came to bring peace on earth? No, I tell you, but division. From now on there will be five in one family divided against each other, three against two and two against three" (Luke 12:51-52).

The Bible frequently uses a sword to symbolize the Word of God (i.e., truth), often in the context of conflict and division. When encouraging the Ephesians to "put on the full armor of God" so they

33

can "stand against the devil's schemes," Paul told them that "the sword of the Spirit ... is the word of God" (Eph. 6:10, 17). The author of Hebrews declares that "the word of God" is "sharper than any double-edged sword," and that "it penetrates even to dividing soul and spirit, joints and marrow" (Heb. 4:12). The book of Revelation depicts a "sharp, double-edged sword" actually "coming out of [Jesus's] mouth," which implies that it represents words or truth (Rev. 1:16). Revelation likewise portrays Jesus threatening to fight the unrepentant "with the sword of [his] mouth" (Rev. 2:16). Why shouldn't we interpret the sword in Matthew 10:34 as another reference to the Word of God, a declaration that Jesus came to bring and wield the truth?[1]

Experience confirms that the gospel message can be divisive. Loving your enemies, for example, often angers your allies. It's often interpreted as an act of disloyalty and can divide those who are united primarily by their common opposition to someone or something. If you doubt this, express love for your nation's enemies and observe how most of your fellow countrymen react. The same goes for family bonds: ask a Christian convert born into a family of Muslims, Hindus, or Buddhists what impact their conversion had on those relationships.

The intermediate context reveals that Jesus made this statement in the middle of preparing his disciples to take his message into the wider world. He was warning them about the personal sacrifices they would have to make to fulfill their mission. Just a few verses earlier, he had told them he was sending them "out like sheep among wolves" (v. 16), instructed them not to fear "those who kill the body but cannot kill the soul" (v. 28), and warned them they would be hated and violently persecuted (vv. 17, 22).[2] Now he was telling them that discipleship could also cost them their families, and maybe even their lives.

Therefore, as Hays observes, "If we are to think at all of any literal sword ... we will immediately see that the disciples of Jesus are to be its victims rather than its wielders."[3] David W. Bercot explains: "Sheep don't carry swords, and they don't slay wolves. Rather, it's the wolves that do the slaying. Jesus was telling His apostles that they needed to be ready to die for Him."[4]

Jesus prioritized the gospel message above everything else, even familial and social peace. He declared the embodiment of God's kingdom, not relational harmony or social stability, to be the highest ideal. He proclaimed that he came to bear witness to the truth, not to absolve all conflict by whatever means necessary. Jesus was and is concerned with establishing true peace on earth through reconciliation, not with imposing the shallow, fleeting peace that results from violent control. This is why Paul writes, "*If it is possible, as far as it depends on you, live at peace with everyone*" (Rom. 12:18). Sometimes peace isn't desirable—for instance, when it requires denying the gospel or collaborating with injustice.

Of course, Jesus wasn't encouraging division. He was only pointing out that pledging supreme allegiance to his kingdom would occasionally produce it. Jim Forest summarizes:

> The "sword" referred to here is not a deadly weapon but a symbol of the fractures that often occur within families and between friends when one chooses to live a life shaped by the Gospel. Jesus is ... saying that the way of life he proposes will at times be a cause of discord that may even cut into the closest relationships.[5]

Everything else Jesus says and does (the broad context of this quote) also reveals he isn't speaking about a literal sword. Nothing in the Bible indicates Jesus ever even touched a sword during his life, let alone came for the purpose of using one. As Hays notes, Jesus's statement about bringing a sword must be interpreted "within the story of a Messiah who refuses the defense of the sword and dies at the hands of a pagan state that bears the power of the sword. The whole New Testament comes rightly into focus only within this story."[6]

Jesus used similar figurative hyperbole on many other occasions to stress the radical commitment he requires of his followers: "If your right eye causes you to stumble, gouge it out and throw it away.... And if your right hand causes you to stumble, cut it off and throw it away" (Matt. 5:29-30).[7] "And do not call anyone on earth 'father,' for you have one Father, and he is in heaven" (Matt. 23:9). "Again I tell you, it is easier for a camel to go through the eye of a needle than for someone who is rich to enter the kingdom of God" (Matt. 19:24). "[Jesus] said to another man, 'Follow me.' But he replied, 'Lord, first let me go and bury my father.' Jesus said to him, 'Let the dead bury their own dead, but you go and proclaim the kingdom of God'" (Luke 9:59-60).[8]

Jesus's statement about hating our family and life may be the most instructive: "If anyone comes to me and does not hate father and mother, wife and children, brothers and sisters—yes, even their own life—such a person cannot be my disciple. And whoever does not carry their cross and follow me cannot be my disciple" (Luke 14:26-27). Jesus didn't want us to literally abhor our families or lives. He wasn't overturning the Fifth Commandment to honor our parents, which he and Paul both affirmed elsewhere.[9] Instead, he was speaking about priorities, about total commitment and the cost of discipleship. He used the verb *hate* not to encourage hostility but to warn against developing idolatrous loyalties.

Accordingly, just as Jesus's instruction to hate our families and lives was a hyperbolic and figurative demand for total allegiance, so was his declaration that he came to bring not peace but a sword. He didn't bring a literal sword of violence. He brought a figurative sword of prioritization.

Lastly, even if we interpret Jesus's sword statement literally, it still doesn't justify our use of violence. If we are going to ignore all context and be literal, let's be literal. Jesus was talking about *his* use of the sword, not ours. He said *he* came to earth to bring a sword, not teach us to use one. In fact, he didn't even say he came to *use* a sword. He said he came to *bring* one. Furthermore, he came to bring only a sword, not knives, guns, nunchucks, or bombs. He said *sword*, not *weapons*. And he came to bring a sword for the purpose of dividing families—nothing else.

Consequently, the only way we can get from "Jesus came to bring a sword to divide families" to "Christians may use various types of violent weapons to do things other than divide families" is to ignore the literal interpretation and the actual context of his statement and instead just make something up. As usual, I like how Hays puts it: "To read this verse as a warrant for the use of violence by Christians is to commit an act of extraordinary hermeneutical violence against the text."[10] Or as Greg Boyd writes, "The use of this passage to justify violence rather reflects the extreme exegetical lengths to which people will go to give divine authority to their own violent agendas."[11] Indeed. It's almost like concluding that Psalm 14:1 asserts, "There is no God," although the entire sentence reads "The fool says in his heart, 'There is no God.'"

Regardless of whether we interpret the passage literally or figuratively, it doesn't justify our use of violence. To interpret it literally is to justify Jesus's possession of a sword, not our own use of one. To interpret it non-literally is to invoke its context, which reveals that Jesus wasn't even talking about violence. He was speaking figuratively about the division that proclaiming the truth and prioritizing allegiance to him inevitably cause, even within families. Had he intended to provide a justification for violence, he would have done so much more clearly, particularly in light of the contradictory immediate, intermediate, and broader contexts of his statement.

Go Buy a Sword

Luke 22:36 is another verse that non-pacifists often cite to justify violence. In it, Jesus told his disciples, "If you don't have a sword, sell your cloak and buy one." As usual, despite initial appearances the context refutes a pro-violence interpretation. Here's the statement in its immediate context:

> Then Jesus asked them, "When I sent you without purse, bag or sandals, did you lack anything?"
>
> "Nothing," they answered.
>
> He said to them, "But now if you have a purse, take it, and also a bag; and if you don't have a sword, sell your cloak and buy one. It is written: 'And he was numbered with the transgressors'; and I tell you that this must be fulfilled in me. Yes, what is written about me is reaching its fulfillment."
>
> The disciples said, "See, Lord, here are two swords."
>
> "That's enough!" he replied. (Luke 22:35-38)

Two reasonable interpretations arise from this passage, neither of which condone any violence.

Interpretation #1. It's hard to argue with Jesus's own explicit explanation of why he told his disciples to buy a sword: to fulfill a prophecy. Take another look at what he said immediately after telling his disciples to buy a sword: "It is written: 'And he was numbered with the transgressors;' and I tell you that this must be fulfilled in me. Yes, what is written about me is reaching its fulfillment."

Jesus was quoting from Isaiah 53 wherein the prophet predicts that the Messiah will be a suffering servant who, having done no wrong and committed no violence, will nonetheless be "numbered with transgressors" and consequently bear unjust punishment. Because the Romans only crucified potential threats to the empire, Jesus needed to give them a reason to arrest and crucify him. He needed to appear to be part of a band of sword-wielding outlaws, a member of a group of violent revolutionaries. So he asked the disciples to play the part of criminals by brandishing swords, which they did. In essence, he was saying to them, "I know I've previously asked you to trust me and not carry any equipment (referring to Matthew 10:9) and that worked out well for you, but now the time has come when equipment is necessary, so trust me again and go grab a sword. As prophesied, I've got to be accused of being a criminal and that needs to happen soon."

Therefore, according to Jesus's own words, he was literally instructing his disciples to go buy swords, but only for the limited, immediate purpose of fulfilling a specific prophecy, not to actually use or keep them.

Two other important pieces of context suggest such an interpretation. First, after the disciples produced two swords, Jesus said, "That's enough!" This begs the question: Enough for what? The only way two swords is enough is if Jesus only intended for them to be used to fulfill the prophecy. Two is enough to be accused of being a criminal gang, but it's not enough to equip each of the twelve disciples for their impending journeys.

Second, after the prophecy had been fulfilled, Jesus immediately condemned the use of the sword and reiterated that he had just fulfilled a prophecy. While Jesus was being arrested, one of his disciples drew his sword and cut off a man's ear.[12] Luke's gospel says Jesus reacted by exclaiming "No more of this!" and healing the man's ear (Luke 22:50-51). Matthew's gospel gives a slightly more detailed account of Jesus's reaction:

> "Put your sword back in its place," Jesus said to him, "for all who draw the sword will die by the sword. Do you think I cannot call on my Father, and he will at once put at my disposal more than twelve legions of angels? But how then would the Scriptures be fulfilled that say it must happen in this way?" (Matt. 26:52-54)

The nonviolence implications couldn't be any clearer. Jesus told his disciples to go buy swords to help him fulfill a prophecy, and then just a few hours later after the prophecy is fulfilled, he (1) instructed them to put their swords away, (2) rectified Peter's use of the sword by healing the man's ear, (3) proclaimed that if he wanted to use violence to advance his kingdom on earth he would call down a few legions of angels from heaven, (4) condemned the use of swords in general, and (5) explained that using the swords to prevent his arrest thwarted the whole reason he wanted them to carry swords in the first place: to cause his arrest. These are not the actions of a king who wants his followers to advance his kingdom through violence.

This interpretation seems to rectify Jesus's two contradictory sword instructions quite nicely. To fulfill the prophecy, he needed them to possess swords, so he ordered them to buy some. After the prophecy was fulfilled, he needed them to return to nonviolent business as usual so he ordered them to put their swords away, forever.

Interpretation #2. There's another reasonable, although I believe slightly less plausible, explanation for Jesus's instruction to go buy swords: mission preparation. When Jesus sent the disciples on their first mission, a local and temporary mission to spread the gospel among their fellow Jews, he instructed them not to take any money or luggage with them but to rely on the hospitality of their families, friends, and fellow countrymen.[13] But now Jesus was preparing them for a much different, more permanent, and largely foreign mission: taking the gospel to the Gentiles. So the material nature of their mission had changed. Whereas before they could expect others to take care of them, now they should expect to take care of themselves. Hence Jesus's new instructions: "But now if you have a purse, take it, and also a bag; and if you don't have a sword, sell your cloak and buy one."

Even if Jesus was dispensing advice on how to prepare for their new mission, that doesn't mean he was necessarily giving *literal* advice. There are many reasons to believe that at least the sword instruction wasn't meant to be taken literally. If Jesus literally wanted them to each carry a sword, why did he tell them two swords was enough for twelve people, most of whom were going to different places? Why did Jesus not specify how he wanted them to use the sword, particularly because he had never before issued any instructions on using swords? Why just hours later when Jesus was being arrested did he condemn sword use? Why does the Bible not record the disciples ever carrying or using swords while missionaries to the gentiles? Did the disciples blatantly disobey Jesus, or did they understand he meant something else? Given those blatant contradictions, Jesus likely wasn't giving the disciples literal advice on how to pack for their upcoming travel.

Instead, Jesus was issuing a figurative warning. He was saying, "You completed the first mission in relative comfort and safety, but now you are about to embark on a new mission that will be uncomfortable and dangerous, so brace yourself. Before, you could expect much welcoming and hospitality, but now you must expect rejection and persecution." The purse and bag represented the material hardship they would face (e.g., hunger, thirst, a lack of shelter, etc.) and the sword symbolized the conflict they would encounter. Such a warning would prove prophetic because the biblical account of the disciples' second mission is full of such struggles.[14]

If Jesus was prepping the disciples for their upcoming mission, he was saying "go buy a sword" in the same figurative sense he had said "I come to bring a sword, not peace."

Interpretation #3. There's actually a third reasonable interpretation option: a hybrid of the first two. Maybe Jesus's instructions were part travel advice and part prophecy fulfillment. Perhaps he was giving them advice on what equipment to take on their new mission. Then, needing to fulfill Isaiah's prophecy, the directive pivoted from packing instructions (take a purse and a bag) to prophecy fulfillment instructions (go get a sword right now), both of which he meant to be taken literally but for different purposes. Or maybe the sword served a dual purpose as both a figurative warning and prophecy prop.

As you can see, even if we interpret Jesus's instruction to go buy a sword literally, there are more reasonable and less reasonable literal interpretations. The most reasonable is that he wanted them to purchase a sword solely to fulfill a prophecy. Any literal interpretation that goes beyond that narrow scope ignores all levels of context and reads things into the passage that aren't there.

Plus, if we are going to be strictly literal, Jesus was speaking only to his disciples, not a crowd, and he told them to buy a sword, not use one. Thus, to conclude that this instruction to his inner circle to buy a sword really means that his followers today can use swords is a logical stretch, to say the least. It veers away from a literal interpretation into a nonliteral one while ignoring the contextual evidence that must necessarily inform any nonliteral analysis. If we can't muster the strength to resist what Bradley Jersak calls the "sloppy propensity to literalize metaphors," we should at least literalize them correctly.[15]

Furthermore, the fact that Jesus had to instruct his disciples to buy swords speaks to his *nonviolence*. It implies that his followers, whom he was about to send out into the world, didn't already own swords (why order someone to buy something he already owns?), which in turn suggests Jesus didn't literally want them using swords. If he had, surely he wouldn't have waited until the end of their time together to instruct them on the moral use of violence.

For all of these reasons, Luke 22:36 does not support the Christian use of violence today. Whatever Jesus meant to communicate by instructing his disciples to buy swords, he did not intend for them, or for us, to use them. Tragically, a passage that should be seen as condemning violence has become just one more reminder of how far fallen humans will go to justify their violence.

Encounters With Soldiers

Another piece of biblical evidence frequently cited to justify violence is Jesus's and his followers' encounters with soldiers. The argument goes like this: because they interacted with soldiers in a friendly, sometimes even complimentary manner without condemning their occupation or instructing them to quit the military, they implicitly condoned soldiering, war, or militarism. Here are the three primary passages cited in connection to this claim, beginning with John the Baptist's encounter, followed by Jesus's, and concluding with Luke's:

"What should we do then?" the crowd asked.

John answered, "Anyone who has two shirts should share with the one who has none, and anyone who has food should do the same."

Even tax collectors came to be baptized. "Teacher," they asked, "what should we do?"

"Don't collect any more than you are required to," he told them.

Then some soldiers asked him, "And what should we do?"

He replied, "Don't extort money and don't accuse people falsely— be content with your pay." (Luke 3:10-14)

When Jesus had entered Capernaum, a centurion came to him, asking for help. "Lord," he said, "my servant lies at home paralyzed, suffering terribly."

Jesus said to him, "Shall I come and heal him?"

The centurion replied, "Lord, I do not deserve to have you come under my roof. But just say the word, and my servant will be healed. For I myself am a man under authority, with soldiers under me. I tell this one, 'Go,' and he goes; and that one, 'Come,' and he comes. I say to my servant, 'Do this,' and he does it."

When Jesus heard this, he was amazed and said to those following him, "Truly I tell you, I have not found anyone in Israel with such great faith. I say to you that many will come from the east and the west, and will take their places at the feast with Abraham, Isaac and Jacob in the kingdom of heaven. But the subjects of the kingdom will be thrown outside, into the darkness, where there will be weeping and gnashing of teeth."

Then Jesus said to the centurion, "Go! Let it be done just as you believed it would." And his servant was healed at that moment. (Matt. 8:5-13)[16]

At Caesarea there was a man named Cornelius, a centurion in what was known as the Italian Regiment. He and all his family were devout and God-fearing; he gave generously to those in need and prayed to God regularly. (Acts 10:1-2)

For numerous reasons, these passages do not justify any Christian use of, or participation in, violence. To begin with, none of them say anything positive about soldiering. Neither John nor Jesus nor Luke complimented the soldiers' profession or professional behavior in any way, shape, or form. Instead, Jesus praised the centurion's faith and Luke his devotion to God, his fear of God, his charity, and his habitual prayer to God. In doing so, they both praised wholly nonviolent attributes, ones that have nothing to do with soldiering.

In fact, neither Jesus nor Luke said *anything*, good or bad, about the centurions' profession or professional conduct. Both merely identified the person as a soldier and stopped there. They didn't turn his profession into a topic of discussion or use the encounter as an opportunity to debate the ethical merits of serving as a member of an occupying military force.

John the Baptist, on the other hand, praised nothing about the soldiers but condemned two of their professional practices, both of which were violent. He instructed them to not extort money and to not dispense false accusations. Note that he didn't tell them to use violence for good, to extort money to give to the poor. So yes, maybe John didn't condemn all violence or tell them to leave the military when he had the chance, but he did condemn two specific violent behaviors, ones that might have made it practically impossible for them to continue being soldiers had they followed his advice. And maybe it did. Maybe they obeyed him and doing so caused them to quit. The Bible doesn't say.

Also bear in mind that John's encounter with the soldiers occurred prior to Jesus's public ministry, so the full extent of Jesus's nonviolent message had not yet been revealed. John knew almost nothing of Christian ethics. Perhaps that's why he didn't issue a more blanket condemnation of all violence. Or maybe he didn't do so because the two soldiers he was talking to were of the less violent type. Maybe they carried weapons but performed more of a police function, only ever using force to restrain local lawbreakers. The passage doesn't tell us much about them. If anything, the nature of John's comments suggests they may have been more like modern-day police officers than modern-day soldiers. Typically police officers, not soldiers, accuse people of crimes. Typically police officers, not soldiers, enforce taxes and therefore have the opportunity to extort.

It's also worth noting that a few English translations interpret John's words in this passage as a condemnation of all violence. For example, the King James Bible, Webster's Bible Translation, and the English Revised Version all translate John as saying, "Do violence to no man." Similarly, Young's Literal Translation says "Do violence to no one."

Of course, Jesus, John, and Luke all wanted the soldiers they encountered to cease all of their sinning in every area of their lives, but condemning their shortcomings wasn't the point of the interactions. Jesus and Luke condemned nothing, and John only condemned two behaviors because the soldiers asked him to. Surely Jesus and Luke didn't intend for their lack of condemnation to imply that the soldiers were sinless or to be read as endorsing everything the soldiers did. Surely John wasn't providing a comprehensive list of everything the soldiers needed to change to achieve perfect righteousness.[17] It is well known that part of an ancient Roman soldier's normal duties included taking part in various pagan ceremonies and other idolatrous practices, but Jesus, John, and Luke never condemned the soldiers for that.[18] Surely their silence as to all the other sinful behaviors the soldiers regularly engaged in, whether personal or professional, wasn't an endorsement of those behaviors. So why do we think it was an endorsement of violence?

Likewise, Jesus interacted with many other sinners in a similar manner, but we don't interpret those encounters as endorsing their lifestyles, behaviors, or professions. For example, when a known sinner washed Jesus's feet with her hair, the Pharisees rebuked her while Jesus welcomed her and complimented her faith, all without condemning her.[19] Jesus interacted with a Samaritan woman who had been divorced five times and was living with a man who was not her husband, but he didn't condemn her for those things.[20] Jesus told the temple priests that "the tax collectors and the prostitutes are entering the kingdom of God ahead of you" (Matt. 21:31). Jesus invited a violent zealot named Simon to be one of his twelve disciples, a member of his inner circle and one of the few who would represent him to the wider world after his death, but there's no evidence Jesus first made it known what he thought about Simon's profession. And as far as we know, Jesus never even condemned the soldiers who crucified him.[21] "In fact, with the exception of the Jewish leaders of his day," notes Boyd, "Jesus never pointed out the things that he did not condone in other people's lives."[22]

So should we conclude that Jesus endorsed sexual promiscuity, serial divorce, tax exploitation, prostitution, violent religious zealotry, and the crucifixion of innocent people? Obviously not. If Luke had identified Cornelius as a member of a well-known band of thieves instead of as a centurion in the Italian Regiment, no one would suggest he had endorsed organized crime. But if we applied the same method of interpretation as those who believe the soldier encounters endorse violence, we would have to.

Put yourself in Jesus's sandals for a moment. Have you ever been friendly to and complimentary of a known sinner without condemning their well-known sin? Ever spoken an encouraging word to someone you knew had just been caught committing adultery or someone who was engaged in a publicly visible struggle with another sin? By not condemning their known sin, did you intend to endorse it? [23]

Jesus's welcoming, encouraging, and loving posture toward all types of sinners was not an endorsement of any sinner's immoral behavior or profession. Instead, it was a demonstration of how to love others, even enemies. Roman soldiers were, after all, a prominent adversary of the Jewish people.

By praising the soldiers' positive attributes and not condemning their negative ones (unless asked to do so), Jesus, John, and Luke were also practicing effective evangelism. Remember, they were welcoming and encouraging potential converts, not engaging veteran believers in nuanced ethical discussions. The two call for different approaches. Searching and seeking must be fostered with compliments, not discouraged with rebukes. Wise evangelism finds common ground, praises it, and establishes a loving relationship *before* it broaches the subject of condemnable conduct. It meets people where they are and focuses on the fundamentals, like faith, which lay the foundation for behavioral change. Condemning someone first only turns them off, makes them defensive, and further alienates them.

Jesus's approach to evangelism was a key difference between him and the Pharisees. While the Pharisees unhesitatingly condemned strangers for their sinful lifestyles, Jesus went out of his way *not* to. The Pharisees rejected people until they cleaned up their act, but Jesus welcomed them as they were, broken and imperfect. Jesus didn't reserve his love for those who *appeared* to have their act together. That's why the tax collectors, prostitutes, and sinners were drawn to him and why he spent so much time with them. On more than one occasion, the Pharisees condemned Jesus for how frequently and non-judgmentally he interacted with such sinners, even going so far as accusing him of gluttony and drunkenness.[24]

Simply put, we should view Jesus's refusal to condemn the soldiers' profession as good evangelism, not as endorsing violence. He refrained from condemning it not because he approved of it but because he knew condemnation would have been counterproductive at that stage in the soldier's faith journey.

This whole situation is ironic. We all recognize that the Pharisees were wrong to accuse Jesus of endorsing things like prostitution, drunkenness, gluttony, and exploitative taxation just because he welcomed, encouraged, and mingled with such people without condemning their sinful behaviors and lifestyles. But those who interpret Jesus, John, and Luke as endorsing violence, soldiering, or militarism because they praised the faith of a soldier without condemning his sinful behavior or lifestyle are making the same mistake. Like the Pharisees, they are erroneously associating Jesus and his disciples with the sinful behaviors of the fallen, broken, searching individuals they embraced and nurtured.

Indeed, one purpose of these soldier encounters was to condemn the Pharisaical way of viewing the world and do what Jesus did on so many occasions: turn commonly accepted power dynamics and prejudices upside down. Jesus was proclaiming that the gospel doesn't discriminate, that it welcomes all, that no one is unredeemable, and that it can reach and change even the unlikeliest types of people—even soldiers. Jesus had made that same point regarding tax collectors and prostitutes when he told the religious leaders in the temple that such people were entering the kingdom of God ahead of them.[25] Now he was making the point with another despised group: Roman occupiers.

Notice whom Jesus was directly addressing when he praised the centurion's faith. It wasn't the centurion—it was the crowd of Israelites following him. He turned to them and said, "Truly I tell you, I have not found anyone *in Israel* with such great faith." Then he informed the crowd that many of the people they think are not a part of God's kingdom, are, and many who think they are, aren't. Jesus was juxtaposing the faith of "outsiders" against the faith of the self-proclaimed "insiders." He was putting the self-righteous Israelites in their place and condemning their prejudices. He was breaking down the antiquated religious barriers between Jews and Gentiles. In other words, he identified the centurion as a soldier to establish him as a despised outsider, not to praise soldiering or endorse violence.

One more observation before we move on. This one is about correct argumentation: To conclude that Jesus's silence about the soldier's profession was an endorsement of violence is to make an argument from silence. It is to deduce a conclusion from what isn't said, to interpret his silence as something more than mere silence, as a message.

Arguments from silence are risky business. More often than not, they are fallacious. So often, in fact, there's an official logical fallacy called the Argument from Silence Fallacy.

To be legitimate, an argument from silence must be supported by overwhelming contextual evidence. The surrounding circumstances must strongly suggest that the silence is saying something. For example, when a politician who is known for his transparent honesty, no matter the cost, and for aggressively denying all false accusations, is unexpectedly asked during a press conference whether he's had an affair and he responds by frowning, shamefully lowering his head, and somberly walking off stage without saying a word, it's reasonable to conclude that his silence communicated an affirmative answer. Even then, however, such an interpretation is rebuttable if additional context can provide a better explanation for his silence. Maybe he hadn't even heard the question because he was preoccupied with reading a text on his phone that was sitting on the podium, a distracting text informing him his child had just been involved in a serious car wreck.

Without overwhelming contextual evidence, an argument from silence can justify anything, as Andy Alexis-Baker explains:

> Since Jesus did not rebuke Pilate for being a governor of an occupying force, he must have sanctioned the Roman occupation and their right to exploit weaker nations, and by extension all colonial and military expansions. Since he did not ask Zacchaeus to leave his job as a tax collector, he must have approved of Roman tax collection and their right to drain resources from an area to the wealthy elite in Rome. Since Jesus did not admonish Pilate for murdering some Galileans in the midst of their sacrifices (Luke 13:3), he sanctioned police brutality and severe repressive measures. Since Jesus did not tell the judges at his own trial that they were wrong for their irregular court proceedings, he sanctions kangaroo courts and dictatorships today. Since Jesus did not reprove the centurion for owning slaves, he therefore condones slavery, even today. These arguments from silence can make Jesus

to be the advocate of whatever we want.... The point is that we have to base our analysis of this text on what Jesus says to the centurion, on the entire narrative that Matthew weaves, and even more broadly, on the picture that the New Testament paints of Jesus in regard to nonviolence.[26]

In our situation, there's *no* contextual evidence to support an endorsement of soldiering, violence, or militarism. Nothing else Jesus, John, or Luke said or did in the immediate context or throughout the rest of the New Testament suggests that they were endorsing or ever had endorsed such things.

On the contrary, when we look at the broader context, which we are in the midst of doing in this book, the evidence suggests a contradictory conclusion: Jesus and his disciples not only didn't endorse violence, but they actually condemned it. For that matter, if there's a valid argument from silence to be made here, it's that Jesus's silence regarding the soldier's profession was a condemnation of it, not an endorsement. Jesus entered the encounter with an antiviolence reputation. Had he wanted to amend his reputation into something less than complete antiviolence, this was the perfect opportunity. That he chose not to compliment the soldier's profession in an otherwise friendly and complimentary encounter implies that he didn't approve of it. That he didn't seize this easy opportunity to qualify his total pacifism is further evidence of his total pacifism.

Here's another way to look at the self-defeating nature of an argument from silence in this situation. No one argues that Jesus's, John's, or Luke's silence endorsed all types of soldiering, violence, and war. Even those who suggest they generally endorsed soldiering as a profession don't claim they endorsed all types of soldiering, like participation in genocidal conquest. So here's the problem: the only way to know where to draw the line between the types of soldiering their silence endorsed and the types it didn't endorse is to bring context into our analysis. And when we look at the context in this situation, we are forced to conclude that their silence wasn't an endorsement at all.

Lasserre made this same point from a slightly different angle. Given that the centurion was a soldier in an *occupying* force, he asked how someone can justify maintaining a *defensive* army if they conclude that Jesus's silence endorsed the centurion's profession:

Those who make so much play with these four "silences," and deduce therefrom that the profession of arms is legitimate, do not seem so keen to deduce that the military occupation of a foreign country is legitimate (seeing that these soldiers had come to Palestine as troops of the occupation). If it *is* legitimate, why do we need a (defensive) army? The justification of military service is destroyed at its roots. And if not, why do they refuse this second deduction, having accepted the first?[27]

Unfortunately, even some of the most prominent theologians to ever live (e.g., Saint Augustine, Thomas Aquinas, and Martin Luther) fell victim to the Argument from Silence Fallacy in their interpretations of these soldier encounters. Nonetheless, the encounters do not justify violence. Jesus didn't endorse everything he didn't condemn. He endorsed only what he said he endorsed: faith. Concluding otherwise is a classic case of reading too much of our own fallen agenda into a situation where it doesn't belong.

There are a dozen lessons to be learned from the soldier encounters, but compatibility of soldiering and violence with the way of Jesus is not one of them.

Jesus's Teachings Summarized

Jesus didn't train his followers on how to morally or properly use violence. He didn't educate them on the difference between just and unjust violence, nor did he instruct them in how to satisfy the "just war" criteria. In fact, he never commanded anyone to use any violence for any reason. He never even implicitly condoned violence. The passages often cited to prove otherwise don't even address the ethics of violence, let alone promote its use.

Jesus taught his followers to refrain from violence. All violence. Always. Even against their enemies, his enemies, and evil itself. Then he went even further! He went beyond prohibiting violence and commanded us to combat evil with loving, self-sacrificial acts of service.

Thus, all of Jesus's commands and other teachings, from his sermons to his interactions with his disciples, send a clear, strong, and consistent antiviolence message.

---

[1] David W. Bercot also points out that in ancient times, "a sword served two purposes," one being "the use we normally think of … in warfare,

where the sword was used for killing" and the other being "a tool for cutting or dividing." See *The Kingdom that Turned the World Upside Down* (Scroll Publishing Company, 2003), 1325, Kindle.

[2] See also Matt. 24:9; John 15:20; Luke 21:12, 16-17; and Mark 13:13.

[3] Hays, *The Moral Vision of the New Testament*, 9315.

[4] David W. Bercot, *The Kingdom that Turned the World Upside Down* (Scroll Publishing Company, 2003), 1325, Kindle.

[5] Jim Forest, *Loving Our Enemies: Reflections on the Hardest Commandment* (Orbis Books, 2014), 2452, Kindle.

[6] Hays, *The Moral Vision of the New Testament*, 9451.

[7] See also Matt. 18:9-9 and Mark 9:43-47.

[8] For Matthew's account, see Matt. 8:21-22. For a different but similar encounter, see Luke 9:61-62.

[9] Exod. 20:12; Matt. 15:1-6; 19:1-19; Mark 10:17-19; Luke 18:18-20; Eph. 6:1-3; Col. 3:20.

[10] Hays, *The Moral Vision of the New Testament*, 9318.

[11] Gregory A. Boyd, *The Crucifixion of the Warrior God: Interpreting the Old Testament's Violent Portraits of God in Light of the Cross, Volumes 1 & 2* (Fortress Press, 2017), 13150, Kindle.

[12] Luke 22:50; Matt. 26:51.

[13] Matt. 10:5-14; Mark 6:7-13; Luke 10:1-12.

[14] For example, see 1 Cor. 4:9-13 and 2 Cor. 6:3-10.

[15] Bradley Jersak, *A More Christlike God: A More Beautiful Gospel* (CWR Press, 2015), 2556, Kindle.

[16] See also Luke 7:1-10.

[17] This is the primary difference between the deductions we performed above regarding the nonviolent implications of Jesus's commands and the current situation. In the former case, Jesus gave us a comprehensive list of everything he wants us to do and told us the most (if not only) effective way to advance his kingdom on earth. Yet he never instructed us to use any type of violence for any reason—and instead instructed us to refrain from many specific types of violence. Thus, it's reasonable to deduce that he doesn't want us using violence, ever. In contrast, the encounters with soldiers do not provide a comprehensive list of everything condemnable about soldiers. Jesus, John, and Luke were not even attempting to communicate such information, so we can't reasonably deduce that their failure to condemn soldiering or violence was an endorsement of such things.

[18] Similarly, it is also well known that the Romans used tax revenue to fund much injustice (like the gladiator games in which Christians were

slaughtered and the operation of blatantly idolatrous, cultic temples), but instead of telling the tax collectors to stop collecting taxes, John only instructed them to not collect more than was required, so should we conclude that he endorsed such injustices?

[19] Luke 7:36-50.

[20] John 4:7-26.

[21] Matt. 27:26-35.

[22] Boyd, *The Crucifixion of the Warrior God*, 13244.

[23] It might help to place these encounters in a more relatable, less emotionally charged context. Pretend you've got a pacifistic friend named Frank. One day you are walking through the mall with Frank and you run into Barry, a friend of yours who is a soldier wearing his uniform. You engage in a minute of small chat and then introduce him to Frank. They also chat for a bit, during which Barry reveals he just celebrated twenty years of marriage with his first and only wife. Frank congratulates Barry and then turns to you and says, "Boy, I wish more of my friends were as committed to their wives as Barry is to his. Most of them have already been divorced two or three times." Did Frank endorse Barry's profession or the use of violence? Was Frank's refusal to go out of his way to condemn the profession of a guy he'd just met an implicit approval of it?

[24] Luke 5:29-31; 7:33-34; 15:1-4; 19:1-10; Mark 2:15-17; Matt. 9:10-13; 11:18-19.

[25] Matt. 21:31-32.

[26] Andy Alexis-Baker, *A Faith Not Worth Fighting For: Addressing Commonly Asked Questions about Christian Nonviolence* (The Peaceable Kingdom Series), ed. Tripp York and Justin Bronson Barringer (Cascade Books, 2012), 3658, Kindle.

[27] Lasserre, *War and the Gospel*, 54.

CHAPTER 4

JESUS'S ACTIONS

In this chapter, we will analyze Jesus's actions, including what he did and did not do during his life on earth. We focus on them because they are what the Bible calls us to mimic. Then, in Chapters 6 and 7, we will examine his actions in the book of Revelation.

When it came to violence, Jesus's actions mirrored his teachings. Setting aside the temple-clearing incident for a moment, he never used violence against anyone, not for any reason. In fact, maybe the most striking thing about his life was his complete abstention from violence.

Jesus had the ability and opportunity to use violence to advance his agenda, but he didn't. He could have chosen the path of a violent zealot or a typical violence-wielding earthly king, but he abstained. When an admiring crowd wanted to turn him into such a king, he fled.[1] When Satan offered him all the political power in the world, he declined.[2] He could have used supernatural violence whenever he wanted, but he never did. Although legions of angels were standing at the ready, he refused to employ them.[3] Despite all the material good he seemingly could have accomplished with it, he *never* used violence to advance God's kingdom on earth.

Jesus didn't even use violence to defend himself. When violence and injustice were done to him, he could have responded with justified physical force, but he refrained. Sometimes he fled violence and other times he endured it, but he never replied in kind.[4] "When they hurled their insults at him, he did not retaliate; when he suffered, he made no threats. Instead, he entrusted himself to him who judges justly" (1 Pet. 2:23). Rather than physically resist violence, Jesus either avoided or absorbed it.

Jesus also never used physical force to defend the innocent, stop injustice, protect religious freedom, or ensure the poor were fed. He never employed violence in the name of love or justice. He was fanatically nonviolent, extreme enough to offend both right-wing nationalists and left-wing communists—and everyone in between.

Physical force was simply not part of Jesus's game plan. He didn't force people to obey his commands, but let them walk away.[5] He didn't force those who had much to give much, but *asked* them to.[6] He didn't force others to serve, but he himself served and then *invited* others to join him. Jesus doesn't even force his way into our hearts and souls. He stands at the door and knocks, hoping we will let him in. But if we don't, he doesn't break the door down.[7] Violence isn't his Plan B. There is no Plan B. There is only Plan A. There is only nonviolence.

The Cross

Jesus's radical nonviolence was most clearly and powerfully demonstrated in his most important act: his crucifixion. All of his words and deeds—his lifetime of perfect self-sacrificial love— culminated in the cross. It was his defining moment, the supreme expression of everything he was about, the climax of his saving work, and the event around which his entire life revolved.[8]

Equally important, the Bible tells us that the cross defines Christian love. "This is how we know what love is: Jesus Christ laid down his life for us" (1 John 3:16). "This is love: not that we loved God, but that he loved us and sent his Son as an atoning sacrifice for our sins" (1 John 4:10). "Greater love has no one than this: to lay down one's life for one's friends" (John 15:13).

Furthermore, the cross defines love as nonviolently as possible. Instead of forcefully defending himself against unjust capital punishment, Jesus voluntarily died a slow, agonizing death. And he did so not only for his family and friends, but for everyone, including his enemies. It doesn't get any more nonviolent than to make the greatest possible sacrifice—your very life—for those who hate you enough to torture you to death. That's the ultimate display of nonviolence. Better yet, it's the precise opposite of violence.

On the cross, Jesus made known the extraordinary extent of his nonviolence. He revealed its inflexible, unwavering, and uncompromising nature. Jesus's death is where everything he was about came together and expressed itself in the ultimate act of nonviolent, other-oriented, enemy-embracing, self-sacrificial love.

Of course, Jesus was doing much more on the cross than teaching nonviolence, but he was still teaching nonviolence. The cross wasn't just something he did for us. It was an example he set for us. It wasn't just theological; it was ethical.

To put it another way, the cross defines how to behave Christianly—i.e., how to obey Jesus, how to do God's will, how to fulfill our purpose, how to advance God's kingdom on earth, etc. Jesus proclaimed, "Whoever wants to be my disciple must deny themselves and take up their cross and follow me. For whoever wants to save their life will lose it, but whoever loses their life for me will find it" (Matt. 16:24-25).[9] "Whoever does not take up their cross and follow me is not worthy of me" (Matt. 10:38). "And whoever does not carry their cross and follow me cannot be my disciple" (Luke 14:27). Notice Jesus didn't say to "believe in" or "talk about" or "worship" the cross. He said to "take up" and "carry" it.

Jesus's apostles taught the same lessons. "Jesus Christ laid down his life for us. And we ought to lay down our lives for our brothers and sisters" (1 John 3:16). "This is love: not that we loved God, but that he loved us and sent his Son as an atoning sacrifice for our sins. Dear friends, since God so loved us, we also ought to love one another" (1 John 4:10-11). "In your relationships with one another, have the same mindset as Christ Jesus ... who made himself nothing by taking the very nature of a servant ... and humbled himself by becoming obedient to death—even death on a cross!" (Phil. 2:5-8). "To this you were called, because Christ suffered for you, leaving you an example that you should follow in his steps" (1 Pet. 2:21). "Husbands, love your wives, just as Christ loved the church and gave himself up for her" (Eph. 5:25). These are just a few examples. There are more.[10]

Jesus's death on the cross instructs us to self-sacrificially absorb violence instead of forcefully resisting it, or worse, inflicting it. It tells us to suffer violence, to allow it to do its worst to us, rather than to use it ourselves.

Cleansing the Temple

Those who insist that Jesus was not a pacifist refer, more than anything else he said or did, to his cleansing of the temple. Here's the incident as it appears in each of the four Gospels:

> Jesus entered the temple courts and drove out all who were buying and selling there. He overturned the tables of the money changers

and the benches of those selling doves. "It is written," he said to them, "'My house will be called a house of prayer,' but you are making it 'a den of robbers.'" (Matt. 21:12-13)

On reaching Jerusalem, Jesus entered the temple courts and began driving out those who were buying and selling there. He overturned the tables of the money changers and the benches of those selling doves, and would not allow anyone to carry merchandise through the temple courts. And as he taught them, he said, "Is it not written: 'My house will be called a house of prayer for all nations'? But you have made it 'a den of robbers.'" (Mark 11:15-17)

When Jesus entered the temple courts, he began to drive out those who were selling. "It is written," he said to them, "'My house will be a house of prayer'; but you have made it 'a den of robbers.'" (Luke 19:45-46)

In the temple courts [Jesus] found people selling cattle, sheep and doves, and others sitting at tables exchanging money. So he made a whip out of cords, and drove all from the temple courts, both sheep and cattle; he scattered the coins of the money changers and overturned their tables. To those who sold doves he said, "Get these out of here! Stop turning my Father's house into a market!" His disciples remembered that it is written: "Zeal for your house will consume me." (John 2:14-17)

Some argue that these physically forceful actions by Jesus himself prove that some violence is morally acceptable, if not commendable. Not so fast. As usual, a little context is in order.

Because too many interpreters jump to conclusions about what Jesus did in these passages, let's begin our analysis by reviewing what the text actually describes. Only *one* of the four accounts (John's, which was written decades after the others) mentions a whip. It also says Jesus made it himself and used it against the livestock only, not against humans. In fact, the only account to mention a whip is also the only account to mention animals. Thus, the "whip" was a homemade herding instrument made on the spot and out of rope, not an Indiana-Jones-like violent weapon.[11] Furthermore, the text doesn't say that Jesus struck the animals. It says he "drove" them out. He could have done so by simply cracking the whip against the ground. In any event, the point was to move the animals, not harm them. (And by moving them, he may have even saved a few from sacrificial death.)

All four accounts say Jesus "drove out" those who were buying and selling in the temple by overturning the money changers' tables and the benches of those selling doves. Mark also mentions that Jesus wouldn't "allow anyone to carry merchandise through the temple courts." Although Jesus used physical force, there's no mention of him striking anyone (or even threatening to) and no mention of any person or animal getting hurt. Herding animals and overturning tables was as "violent" as Jesus got. This suggests he drove the buyers and sellers out primarily by the force of his moral authority, not violence. He couldn't have been too physically threatening because the armed temple guards never intervened, let alone arrested him.

To the extent that there's a moral distinction to be drawn between aggressive and reactive force, there's substantial textual evidence that suggests Jesus's physical force was wholly reactive. In each of the four accounts, Jesus refers to the temple as his or his father's house. In doing so, he obviously wasn't claiming that he and God possessed a legal deed issued by the Roman government, but there is a sense in which the temple was their property. In reality, their moral right to it was infinitely superior to the authority of any earthly legal document. Throughout Israel's history, the temple was known as God's house on earth and was always governed by special God-given rules regarding who could enter, when they could enter, and what they could do once inside, with harsh penalties for even the slightest violations.

From this perspective, Jesus was merely, and reactively, expelling unwanted trespassers from his property. The merchants were the aggressors because they had entered his house and violated his rules. They had turned it into a market and were defrauding people. Plus, according to the text, Jesus directed his actions at such aggressors— the money changers, dove sellers, and those carrying merchandise.

The presence of fraud is revealing. In Jesus's day, the use of false weights to defraud people when exchanging money was an all-too-common practice. So was the charging of exploitatively high exchange rates. There's even historical evidence to suggest that some priests were in on the action. They required the temple tax to be paid in temple coins and had a monopoly on issuing such coins, which they occasionally manipulated to benefit themselves at the worshipers' expense. Likewise, some priests were exploiting the temple's sacrificial system for their own financial benefit. They would confiscate a worshiper's animal under the pretense that it wasn't pure enough to sacrifice, and then they'd turn around and sell it to another worshiper further down the line. From this perspective, Jesus was reactively combating aggressive acts of fraud and exploitation. He was "cleansing" the temple of violent economic practices. And as such, his actions were antiviolence.[12]

As usual, it's also hard to argue with Jesus's own explanation of his actions. In regards to his actions in the temple, his explanation revolves around prophetic symbolism. In three of the four accounts, he followed up his actions by proclaiming, "It is written, 'My house will be called a house of prayer,' but you are making it 'a den of robbers.'" Jesus was referring to Isaiah 56:7 and Jeremiah 7:11. Hays explains their significance:

> The first of these ("My house shall be called a house of prayer for all the nations") evokes the eschatological vision of Isaiah 55–66 in which God will restore and redeem Jerusalem, bringing all nations to worship God truly there. An integral part of that vision is the abolition of violence, as symbolized by the peaceful coexistence of the wolf and the lamb and the promise that "they shall not hurt or destroy on all my holy mountain" (Isa. 65:25). The other phrase ("You have made it a den of robbers") is an allusion to Jeremiah's Temple Sermon (Jer. 7:1–15), a vehement call for repentance that condemns Israel for stealing, murder, adultery, false swearing, and idolatry. To continue the charade of Temple worship while committing these offenses is to "trust in deceptive words to no avail" (Jer. 7:8).[13]

Likewise, in the remaining account, John notes that Jesus's "disciples remembered that it is written: 'Zeal for your house will consume me.'" Here's Hays again:

> John, citing Psalm 69:9 … reads the story as prefiguring Jesus's death; additionally, his account of Jesus's words ("Stop making my father's house a marketplace," John 2:16) may allude to Zechariah's apocalyptic vision of the day of the Lord, in which "there shall no longer be traders in the house of the Lord of hosts" (Zech. 14:21).[14]

If we interpret Jesus's actions from his own explicitly stated perspective, they must be understood as symbolic acts of prophecy, not as an ethical lesson on the proper use of physical force. Jesus was, to quote Hays once more, engaging in "an act of 'street theater,' in line with precedents well established in Israel's prophetic tradition" and therefore his temple actions should be understood "as a call for repentance and a sign that the promised eschatological restoration is at hand."[15]

Speaking of prophecies, the Old Testament prophet Isaiah apparently didn't believe Jesus's actions in the temple constituted violence. He prophesied the Messiah would be "assigned a grave with the wicked ... *though he had done no violence*" (Isa. 53:9).

Even Jesus's audience seemed to understand the symbolic nature of his actions. Their reactions centered on questioning Jesus's authority to act as he had, not on the physical nature of his actions. Mark's account, for example, says that the religious leaders scolded Jesus for claiming authority he didn't possess, not for being violent or injuring people.[16] Similarly, John's account indicates that the Jews questioned Jesus's authority, not his use of physical force.[17] And there's no record of anyone accusing Jesus of hypocrisy, of contradicting all of his earlier nonviolent instructions, like his command to turn the other cheek.[18] No one involved in the temple incident viewed it as the moment in which Jesus's pacifism was disproven.

Furthermore, it appears to have been a *premeditated* symbolic act, not an uncontrolled, spur-of-the-moment fit of rage. As Boyd has pointed out, "Most New Testament scholars concur that this was a calculated, strategic act on Jesus's part," one that "contained deep symbolic significance."[19] Scholars disagree on precisely what Jesus was symbolizing (his identity as the long-awaited Messiah, the economic corruption of the temple system, the removal of the temple as a middleman between individuals and God, apocalyptic eschatology, final judgment, etc.), but "they all presuppose that the temple cleansing was anything but a spontaneous tantrum on the part of Jesus."[20]

According to Christian peace activist John Dear, Jesus's actions are best described as "a classic example of symbolic, nonviolent direct action."[21]

> Mark's version (11:11–26) notes that Jesus first entered the temple, looked around, left, returned the next day and then took action. Only those who have undertaken civil disobedience with a steadfast commitment to nonviolence could understand that sentence: Jesus was casing the joint! He wanted to see for himself

what was happening, plan his action, pray over it, and be perfectly nonviolent.[22]

Jesus didn't enter the temple to demonstrate the moral acceptability of violence. Precisely the opposite—like an antiwar protestor who enters a military facility to pour blood on a warship, he entered the temple to engage in strategic nonviolent activism against the use of violence. He employed symbolic violence to condemn the real violence of the temple system. As such, the incident is further proof that Jesus wasn't nonresistant but was instead nonviolently resistant.[23]

We must never forget that Jesus was a passionate human being who cared deeply about justice and who devoted himself to *proactively* advancing God's kingdom on earth. He wasn't passive toward evil; he was at war with it. Dear comments further:

> [Jesus] did not sit under a tree and practice his breathing. He walked regularly into the face of danger, spoke the truth, and demanded justice. As far as decent, law-abiding, religious people were concerned, he was nothing but trouble. He hung out with the wrong people, healed at the wrong time, visited the wrong places, and said the wrong things. His nonviolence was active, provocative, public, daring, and dangerous. Most of Jesus's actions were illegal. He committed civil disobedience on an almost daily basis.[24]

Besides being a symbolic act of prophecy, many scholars also theorize that Jesus's actions performed another, more practical purpose: the hastening of his crucifixion. His actions were, after all, blatantly threatening to the political and religious authorities. Thomas R. Yoder Neufeld suggests "his contemporaries would have perceived prophetic words of condemnation as far graver and more fearsome than any use of a whip made of the straw lying around."[25] Mark and Luke both state that the incident caused the chief priests and teachers of the law to immediately begin looking for a way to kill Jesus.[26] In fact, Jesus was arrested and executed shortly thereafter. So whether or not Jesus consciously intended to accelerate his inevitable persecution, it seemed to have that effect.[27]

Even if we insist, against Jesus's intent, on interpreting his actions as a lesson on how to morally use physical force, those actions only justify a very narrow, very specific type of *reactive* force. Precisely what type depends upon how literal we get. The most strictly literal reading would conclude that his example only justifies a single use of mild, brief, indirect, non-weaponized, non-injurious reactive physical force (the type that overturns a few tables and scatters a few animals) within a place of worship for the purpose of prophetic symbolism. A less literal reading, on the other hand, could justify much more general forms of reactive force. In any event, it's difficult to find much textual support for the use of reactive force that harms others, let alone justifies war. Wars aren't fought with homemade herding instruments and impassioned prophetic announcements.

The problem, as always, is that once we ignore the context enough that we can treat the incident as an ethical lesson, there's nothing left to prevent us from jumping to all sorts of unsupported (and even textually contradicted) conclusions. In fact, once you disregard context in any degree, you've started down a slippery slope to justifying whatever suits your fancy, and what inevitably results is a subjective, self-serving interpretation. Adolf Hitler, for example, cited this very incident to justify not only violence but ethnic violence against Jews:

> My feelings as a Christian point me to my Lord and Savior as a fighter. It points me to the man who once in loneliness, surrounded by a few followers, recognized these Jews for what they were and summoned men to fight against them and who, God's truth!, was greatest not as a sufferer but as a fighter. In boundless love as a Christian and as a man I read through the passage which tells us how the Lord at last rose in His might and seized the scourge to drive out of the Temple the brood of vipers and adders. How terrific was His fight for the world against the Jewish poison.[28]

When we consider the *entire* context, the picture that emerges is wholly nonviolent. For starters, this is the only passage in the entire Bible in which Jesus uses physical force of any kind for any reason. That alone makes a strong case for Christian nonviolence. As a matter of fact, the only reason the incident is so scandalous in the popular mind is because it was so unique, so out of character for Jesus. This is why non-pacifists cite the temple incident so frequently: it's about all they have to work with, at least in regards to his first coming.

And yet it's not even a long passage. John's description is the most detailed and contains only five short sentences. Matthew and Mark devote only three short sentences to it, and Luke just two. The whole incident is basically mentioned in passing, with little detail or explanation. Had Jesus intended his actions in the temple that day to overturn everything else he had said and done (and would continue to say and do), he would have acted much differently, or at least given a better explanation for his use of force. And the Gospel writers would have devoted more ink to their reports. The brevity of their accounts reveals that Jesus's single use of physical force wasn't meant to play a significant role—if any role at all—in defining Christian ethics.

Instead of interpreting the rest of Jesus's life in light of the temple incident, we must interpret the temple incident in light of the rest of Jesus's life—including the greatest commandment, the Sermon on the Mount, and Jesus's death on a cross. When we do, we discover that the Jesus of the temple does not contradict the loving, self-sacrificing, nonviolent Jesus of the rest of the Bible. Rather, we realize that his temple actions arose out of love for his father's house and his fellow humans, which is why they were designed to keep the temple holy, protect the innocent from exploitation, and warn the corrupt about the imminent consequences of their actions.

Violence Against Nature

There are two instances in which Jesus is accused of using violence against nature, one involving a group of pigs and the other a fig tree. This is a book about violence against humans, so we won't analyze these events in detail. I do, however, want to make two quick observations about each.

In the pig incident, Jesus encounters a demon-possessed man, orders the demons out of him, and, at the demons' request, sends them into a nearby group of pigs, who promptly run into a lake and drown.[29] However, nowhere in any of the three Gospel accounts of this event does it say that Jesus killed the pigs. Why should we assume that Jesus—whom the New Testament shows to be a healer, restorer, and redeemer of life—sent the pigs running into the lake to drown?[30] It makes more sense to conclude that Satan—whom the Bible calls a destroyer, devourer, and murderer—and his demons were the cause. After all, the demons had just been torturing the man they possessed by driving him insane, making him wander around a cemetery naked while screaming and cutting himself.[31] Why wouldn't they have a similarly destructive effect on the pigs?

Even if we could somehow pin the pigs' deaths on Jesus, such an act wouldn't imply that we have no duty of care toward animals, as Saint Augustine and others have suggested. Instead, it indicates that human life should be prioritized over animal life when both can't be protected. It's as if Jesus was saying, "Given the option between saving a human or 2,000 pigs, save the human."[32] But that doesn't mean we shouldn't also try to save the pigs.

If you'd like an insightful explanation of the other violence-mitigating circumstances of this event, including its spiritual warfare context, see Greg Boyd's *Crucifixion of the Warrior God*.[33]

In the fig tree incident, a hungry Jesus approaches a fig tree and, looking for fruit, finds it to be barren. He curses the tree, causing it to wither.[34] First, many scholars interpret this event as a symbolic act of forthcoming judgment (against Jerusalem and the temple system), much like Jesus's temple clearing.[35] The Old Testament prophets often used props in such a way.[36] On many occasions, fig trees were used to symbolize spiritual fruitfulness or unfruitfulness.[37] Thus, like the temple incident, this was a prophetic act with deep symbolic meaning, not a reflexive use of violence born of a temper tantrum. Mark's account even places the temple episode in the middle of this fig tree story, indicating that he intends for them to frame and interpret each other.

Second, the disciples who saw Jesus do this didn't even notice his violence, if the use of force against a barren tree even qualifies as violence. They lived in a world wherein the severe and systematic use of violence against humans, like slavery, was taken for granted as a necessary part of life, so causing a single tree to wither hardly constituted misbehavior. What the disciples noticed instead was Jesus's miraculous ability to cause the tree to wither so fast, which Jesus used to teach them about the power of faith, saying to them, "if you have faith and do not doubt, not only can you do what was done to the fig tree, but also you can say to this mountain, 'Go, throw yourself into the sea,' and it will be done" (Matt. 21:21).

In any event, citing Jesus's single use of violence against a *tree* to argue that he wasn't a pacifist or to help justify our use of violence against other *humans* is an uninspiring, if not desperate, attempt to come up with supporting evidence for such assertions.

Jesus's Actions Summarized

Not only did Jesus teach complete nonviolence, he lived it. His life and death embodied a literal interpretation of his instructions, given in the Sermon on the Mount and elsewhere.

Jesus's actions in the temple don't refute this conclusion. They don't disqualify him from pacifism, at least not if we apply the same commonly accepted definition of pacifism we apply to everyone else. The Merriam-Webster Dictionary defines pacifism as "opposition to war or violence as a means of settling disputes, specifically refusal to bear arms on moral or religious grounds." Clearly Jesus fits the bill, his single symbolic use of minor physical force against the tables and animals of trespassers and exploiters notwithstanding. Had Gandhi or Martin Luther King, Jr. once engaged in a similar act, no reasonable interpreter would argue that it proved he was no longer entirely opposed to violence.

Here's another way to look at it: If an otherwise perfect vegetarian ate a tiny bite of meat one time for an obviously symbolic purpose that had nothing to do with endorsing the eating of meat (and is actually best interpreted as a symbolic act of protest *against* a system corrupted by the eating of meat), would we still consider her a vegetarian? We would, especially if she was later tortured to death because she refused to save herself by eating meat just one more time. We'd label her passionately vegetarian. In the same way, Jesus was passionately pacifistic.

---

[1] John 6:1-15.

[2] Luke 4:5-8.

[3] Matt. 26:52-53.

[4] Matt. 2:13-15; 12:14-15; 26:50-53, 67; 27:29-30, 39-44; Luke 4:28-30; 23:35-39; Mark 3:6-7; John 8:59; 12:36.

[5] Matt. 19:16-22; Mark 10:17-31; Luke 18:18-30.

[6] Luke 12:48.

[7] Rev. 3:20.

[8] Of course, we must also give the resurrection its due. It too is essential and climactic. It proved Jesus truly was God's messenger and our Savior. It

proved the wisdom and power of what he accomplished on the cross. It proved love really does conquer all, even death. It proved we can self-sacrificially love others without fearing death because it doesn't have the last word. So, yes, the resurrection is indispensable, but it didn't change what was revealed on the cross or its centrality. Rather, it verified them.

9 See also Mark 8:34-35 and Luke 9:23-24.

10 Here are a few more: Eph. 5:1-2; Phil. 3:10; Rom. 12:1; 2 Tim. 2:3.

11 According to Eric Seibert, "The word for 'cords' only occurs twice in the New Testament, here and in Acts 27:32. In Acts, it refers to rope used to moor a boat to a dock. Jesus's whip was made of rope, nothing more. It was *not* like a Roman whip, which often had sharp objects embedded in it to inflict maximum pain and harm." See *Disarming the Church: Why Christians Must Forsake Violence to Follow Jesus and Change the World* (Cascade Books, 2018), 2105, Kindle.

12 Anthony W. Bartlett even argues that the word used for "robbers" in this passage is better translated more broadly as "violent men." See *Seven Stories: How to Study and Teach the Nonviolent Bible* (Hopetime Press, 2017), 183, Kindle.

13 Hays, *The Moral Vision of the New Testament*, 9331.

14 Ibid., 9353.

15 Ibid.

16 Mark 11:28.

17 John 2:18.

18 Or as N.T. Wright observes, the Gospel writers all saw that "Jesus's dramatic action was a way of declaring that the Temple was under God's judgment and would, before too long, be destroyed forever," which is why they "follow the incident with a string of discussions that all turn on the question of whether Jesus has the right to do this kind of thing, what he means by it, what sort of a revolution he has in mind, and so on." See *Simply Jesus: A New Vision of Who He Was, What He Did, and Why He Matters* (HarperCollins, 2011), 2219, Kindle.

19 Boyd, *The Crucifixion of the Warrior God*, 5120.

20 Ibid.

21 John Dear, *A Faith Not Worth Fighting For: Addressing Commonly Asked Questions about Christian Nonviolence* (The Peaceable Kingdom Series), ed. Tripp York and Justin Bronson Barringer (Cascade Books, 2012), 3874, Kindle.

22 Ibid.

23 Unfortunately, as is so often the case with divine responses to injustice in the Bible, human interpreters employ a lose-lose perspective. When God

or Jesus doesn't do more to passionately and forcefully combat injustice, he is labeled as passive or uncaring. But the moment he uses force against injustice, even force as mild as Jesus used here, he is called violent or bloodthirsty.

[24] Dear, *A Faith Not Worth Fighting For*, 3856.

[25] Thomas R. Yoder Neufeld, *Killing Enmity: Violence and the New Testament* (Baker Academic, 2011), 1100, Kindle.

[26] Mark 11:18; Luke 19:47-48.

[27] In this regard, Jesus' temple actions served the same purpose as his instructions to his disciples to go buy a sword.

[28] From a speech in Munich on April 12, 1922 (Norman H. Baynes, ed. *The Speeches of Adolf Hitler*, April 1922 – August 1939, Vol. 1 of 2, pp. 19-20, Oxford University Press, 1942).

[29] Mark 5:1-20; Luke 8:26-39; Matt. 8:28-34.

[30] The only destructive act directly attributed to Jesus in the entire Bible was his withering of a fig tree, which we are about to analyze.

[31] Mark 5:3-5; Luke 8:27.

[32] Of course, we can't know whether those were Jesus's only two options. We don't know the metaphysics of miracles or spiritual warfare. Given this, it seems reasonable to give the divine Son of the creator of the universe the benefit of the doubt.

[33] More specifically, see Appendix II to Volume 1.

[34] Matt. 21:18-22; Mark 11:12-14, 20-26.

[35] See Chapter 4 in Mark L. Strauss' *Jesus Behaving Badly: The Puzzling Paradoxes of the Man from Galilee* (InterVarsity Press, 2015), which is Kindle location 804 to 917.

[36] Jer. 13:1-11; 19:1-13; 1 Kings 11:29-31; Isa. 20:1-6; Ezek. 4:1-15; Hosea 1:2.

[37] Isa. 28:4; Jer. 8:13; 24:1-10; 29:17; Hosea 2:12; 9:10, 16-17; Mic. 7:1.

CHAPTER 5

VIOLENT METAPHORS, ANALOGIES, AND PARABLES

To properly understand the violent metaphors, analogies, and parables employed by Jesus and others throughout the New Testament, we need to first set the larger biblical context within which they were uttered.

The Biblical Worldview

The Bible contains a *warfare* worldview. It frames reality in terms of a great war between God and Satan, between good and evil, between the kingdom of light and the kingdom of darkness. According to the Bible, the story of the universe is the story of God's creation, Satan's subsequent invasion, and God's gradual restoration of his kingdom, on earth as it is in heaven. Everything in the Bible occurs in this context, from Satan's role in the Garden of Eden to God's final destruction of the beast in Revelation.[1] "There is no neutral ground in the universe," wrote C. S. Lewis. "Every square inch, every split second, is claimed by God and counterclaimed by Satan."[2]

Throughout both Testaments, the Bible uses words like "kingdom," "rule," "dominion," and "sovereignty" to describe what God was doing—through Israel, the prophets, Jesus, the apostles, and the early church. Even the titles that frequently preface the names of God and Jesus are loaded with earthly kingdom implications. The Bible regularly refers to God as "God of gods," "Lord of lords," and "Lord of heaven and earth,"[3] while it similarly calls Jesus "Lord of lords and King of kings."[4]

The Bible establishes Satan as God's adversary, calling him things like "the enemy," "the evil one," and "the prince of demons."[5] And it doesn't merely refer to Satan as *an* enemy or *an* evil one, but as *the* enemy and *the* evil one. Satan and God are so antithetical they are often symbolically contrasted as darkness versus light,[6] with Paul labeling Satan "the dominion of darkness" (Col. 1:13).

The Bible also frequently gives Satan credit for ruling the world, identifying him as "the prince of this world," "the god of this age," and "the ruler of the kingdom of the air."[7] According to 1 John 5:19, "the whole world is under the control of the evil one." And when Satan promised to give Jesus all the kingdoms of the world if he disobeyed God, Jesus didn't question the evil one's possession of them.[8] Furthermore, Satan's power over all nations and people is a prevalent theme throughout the book of Revelation.[9] As Boyd concludes, "while Jesus and his followers of course believed that God was the *ultimate* Lord over creation, it is apparent that Jesus viewed Satan as the *functional* ruler over the earth at the present time."[10]

Throughout the Bible, Satan is engaged in constant conflict with God's kingdom. He has been attempting to thwart it since the beginning.[11] He is "the enemy of everything that is right," "full of all kinds of deceit and trickery," and constantly "perverting the right ways of the Lord" (Acts 13:10). He deceives the nations and leads the entire world astray.[12] "He is a liar" who "masquerades as an angel of light" (John 8:44; 2 Cor. 11:14). He sows strife and incites people to disobey God.[13] He uses sinful desires to enslave us and wage war against our souls and bodies.[14] He blocks believers' attempts to spread the gospel, and he prevents individuals from hearing and understanding God's Word.[15] He "prowls around like a roaring lion looking for someone to devour" (1 Pet. 5:8). Occasionally, he even competes directly against God for the obedience of human beings, including Jesus.[16] "In the Bible," writes Richard Beck, "Satan and the Devil are interchangeable names for the personification of all that is adversarial to the kingdom and people of God, the personified Enemy of God."[17]

Jesus's Nemesis

While Jesus was on earth, he was constantly battling Satan. As soon as Jesus was born, Satan tried to kill him,[18] and immediately after God pronounced Jesus to be the Messiah, Satan engaged him in the wilderness, tempting him with all the kingdoms of the world in exchange for worship.[19] From that day forward, Jesus spent much of his remaining time on earth combating Satan's handiwork by healing those who were under his power, sometimes by curing diseases and other times by casting out demons.[20] Eventually, Satan's evil forces orchestrated Jesus's crucifixion, prompting Judas to betray him.[21] No wonder Jesus called Satan a "murderer from the beginning," the "father of lies," and a "stumbling block to me" (John 8:43-44; Matt. 16:23). As Dietrich Bonhoeffer concluded, "the whole of his life was one long conflict with the devil."[22]

Evidence of this conflict is everywhere in the Gospels. Consider how Jesus's healings and exorcisms are described. They are portrayed as skirmishes in the ongoing war between God's kingdom and Satan's. Through these healings, Jesus was reclaiming captured territory and people. He was restoring the lives that Satan had destroyed, setting people free from the devil's anti-human grip. For "if it is by the Spirit of God that I drive out demons," proclaimed Jesus, "then the kingdom of God has come upon you" (Matt. 12:28). Similarly, when John the Baptist asked Jesus whether he was the promised Messiah, Jesus justified his affirmative claim by pointing to his restorative miracles: "The blind receive sight, the lame walk, those who have leprosy are cleansed, the deaf hear, the dead are raised, and the good news is proclaimed to the poor" (Matt. 11:5).

Jesus came to earth to defeat Satan's rule and set us free from bondage. He came to "destroy the devil's work," condemn him, drive him out, and break his power, including his power in death.[23] He came to replace Satan's kingdom of evil, death, oppression, bloodshed, hatred, vengeance, sickness, poverty, suffering, darkness, temptation, deception, falsehood, and division with God's kingdom of peace, truth, light, joy, beauty, freedom, health, abundance, relationship, brotherhood, and unity. He came to set creation free, to liberate it from enslavement to sin and all of sin's negative effects—psychological, physical, spiritual, social, and environmental.[24] He came to overthrow the tyranny of the devil and render evil powerless, to conquer injustice and restore justice, to eradicate death and give life.

Simply put, Jesus came to earth to advance God's kingdom over and against Satan's. This was the central theme, the primary mission, of his entire life and ministry. He focused all his efforts on turning the kingdom of the world into the kingdom of God. It is why he lived and died and rose again.

Jesus himself declared this to be his purpose: "I must proclaim the good news of the kingdom of God to the other towns also, because that is why I was sent" (Luke 4:43). To proclaim the arrival of God's kingdom was to declare war on Satan's kingdom, including earthly kingdoms that operate through his evil means of violence and power. Labeling this proclamation the "gospel" and "good news" would have made this evident to Jesus's audience, as Frank Viola explains:

> In the first century, the words "gospel" and "evangelize" referred to heralding the good news that a new emperor had been installed in the Roman Empire. Heralds would go out to proclaim the good news, informing people that a new era of peace, salvation, and blessing had begun…. The apostles used this same language to describe the preaching of the gospel of Jesus Christ. The gospel that the apostles preached was the announcement—the heralding—that Jesus of Nazareth had become this world's true Emperor (Lord), launching a new era of peace, salvation, and blessing, and because of it, everything has changed.[25]

Jesus's entire message was unmistakably kingdom-centered. He didn't just preach about God, the good news, or the gospel. He preached about the *kingdom* of God (or as Matthew calls it, the kingdom of heaven),[26] the good news of the *kingdom* of God, and the gospel of the *kingdom*.[27] His arrival marked a fundamental change in the biblical message, from the law and the prophets to the "good news of the kingdom of God" (Luke 16:16).[28] His earliest public announcement was "Repent, for the kingdom of heaven has come near" (Matt. 4:17).

Jesus spoke more about the kingdom of God than about any other topic. He spent his entire ministry talking about it—what it is like, how to enter it, who is and isn't there, who is the greatest in it, how it differs from worldly kingdoms, how it will triumph over all other earthly kingdoms, etc.[29] Even after he was crucified, died, and rose from the dead, he immediately resumed talking about the kingdom of God.[30]

Of course, Jesus also spoke about his dying for our sins, giving us eternal life, and other aspects of personal salvation, but those things, while important, were not his primary message. They were subparts of a larger, more central theme that tied them—and everything else in Scripture—together: the advancement of God's kingdom on earth as it is in heaven.

But don't take my word for it. Open your Bible and check it out. Once you know to look for it, you'll find kingdom talk everywhere.

It permeates the Gospels. The kingdom of God is nothing less than the purpose and goal of human history.

The Victory of the Cross

Jesus's conflict with Satan reached its climax on the cross. To the world, it looked—and still looks—like Satan won. In a world that values control and survival above all else, being tortured to death as a seemingly helpless outcast was a clear and total defeat. In fact, it was about as painful and humiliating of a defeat as possible.

But Christianity proclaims this climatic moment a victory. "And having disarmed the powers and authorities, [Jesus] made a public spectacle of them, triumphing over them by the cross" (Col. 2:15). Jesus "shared in their humanity so that by his death he might break the power of him who holds the power of death—that is, the devil— and free those who all their lives were held in slavery by their fear of death" (Heb. 2:14-15). "The sting of death is sin, and the power of sin is the law. But thanks be to God! He gives us the victory through our Lord Jesus Christ" (1 Cor. 15:56-57). Referring to his own impending death, Jesus said, "Now is the time for judgment on this world; now the prince of this world will be driven out" (John 12:31). After all, "The reason the Son of God appeared was to destroy the devil's work" (1 John 3:8).

However paradoxical it may seem, the entire New Testament declares Jesus's crucifixion a victory over Satan and his kingdom. "Every major strand of the New Testament," writes Yoder, "each in its own way, interprets the acceptance by Jesus of the violence of the cross as the means, necessary and sufficient, of God's victory over the rebellious powers."[31] And as Lee C. Camp observes, "the New Testament closes with this very assertion: that it is the slaughtered Lamb who is worshiped as the victorious one, triumphing over the enemies of God."[32] Jesus accomplished many other things on the cross,[33] but he also, and not least of all, conquered his archenemy, including that enemy's most powerful weapon—death.[34]

Thus, the cross isn't a barrier to, prerequisite for, or consequence of Jesus's victory. It is the victory itself. It is the triumph of good over evil. In other words, it isn't just Jesus who defeated Satan. It is the *crucified* Jesus. He is "now crowned with glory and honor *because* he suffered death" (Heb. 2:9).

Of course, the resurrection is important too. Essential, in fact. But it wasn't the victory; the cross was.[35] The cross was the victory because it is where Jesus's lifetime of perfect love reached its completion and ultimate expression. It is where he endured the worst evil could do to him without straying from the way of love. Jesus triumphed over evil not by rising from the dead but by always loving (and remaining nonviolent), even unto death. The resurrection simply proved it. Strictly speaking, the cross was the victory and the resurrection was the vindication of (and reward for) that victory.

To describe the victory in slightly different terms, by his death and resurrection Jesus became, and remains, king on earth. Because of this victory, he is now in charge. "He is the head over every power and authority" (Col. 2:10). God "raised Christ from the dead and seated him at his right hand in the heavenly realms, far above all rule and authority, power and dominion, and every name that is invoked, not only in the present age but also in the one to come" (Eph. 1:20-21). Jesus is now "at God's right hand—with angels, authorities and powers in submission to him" (1 Pet. 3:22). "All authority in heaven and on earth has been given to me," declared the risen Jesus (Matt. 28:18). Even according to the book of Revelation, Jesus is already— prior to his second coming—"the ruler of the kings of the earth" (Rev. 1:5).[36] The entire New Testament declares it.

N. T. Wright calls this fact "the forgotten story of the gospels."[37] He claims we have almost entirely forgotten that "devastating and challenging message," which "the past two hundred years of European and American culture have been desperately trying to stifle."[38] He's got a point. When is the last time you heard a sermon on Jesus's earthly kingship or the Kingdom of God? Nevertheless, "the story of Jesus is the story of how Israel's God became king on earth," and "the whole point of the gospels" is to tell that story.[39] Indeed, "once you lose the kingdom-theme, which is central to the gospels," Wright adds, "everything else becomes reinterpreted in ways that radically distort" their messages.[40] "The gospels are not about 'how Jesus turned out to be God.' They are about *how God became king on earth as in heaven.*"[41]

That being said, Jesus's victory isn't yet complete. He has initiated his earthly kingship, but he isn't yet earth's sole ruler. Satan still reigns, in part. Nonetheless, Jesus has won a pivotal battle. His life, death, and resurrection set in motion the beginning of the end of Satan's kingdom. Like D-Day in WWII, he didn't end the war between God and Satan but he did strike the decisive blow that determined who will eventually and inevitably win it. Total victory is assured but not yet realized. Sin, death, and evil itself have been conquered, but not yet eradicated.

In this sense, God's kingdom is already, but not yet. It is already here, but not yet fully here. It is present, yet future, which is why Jesus often referred to God's kingdom in the present *and* future tense.[42]

Eventually, Jesus will finish the job. He will bring the future into fulfillment. He will return to earth to annihilate all remaining evil power and finalize God's total and eternal reign.[43] He will complete what he started in the Gospels: the re-establishment of God's kingdom on earth as it is in heaven. If his death and resurrection was D-Day, his second coming will be V-Day, the final victory that will end all conflict, pain, suffering, and death.[44] The whole Bible testifies to this truth, and even the devil knows it.[45]

Analogizing the Christian as Soldier

Here's the point of presenting all this warfare worldview evidence: It explains why Jesus and the New Testament writers employ so many military metaphors. Our Christian purpose is located within this ongoing battle. God has tasked us with continuing the fight, with taking back territory for his kingdom, with spreading his sovereign rule and dominion on earth as it is in heaven. "Enemy-occupied territory—that is what this world is," wrote C.S. Lewis. "Christianity is the story of how the rightful king has landed, you might say landed in disguise, and is calling us to take part in a great campaign of sabotage."[46] "To be a Christian is to be a warrior," concluded Charles H. Spurgeon. "The good soldier of Jesus Christ must not expect to find ease in this world; it is a battlefield."[47]

God's earthly battle against evil rages on and we are an important part of it. To be baptized is to be conscripted into God's army and to join his costly campaign against Satan's violent, destructive, oppressive, exploitative, death-wielding kingdom. As Christians, our occupation is war.

Hence all of the New Testament's soldiering and fighting metaphors. On two occasions, Paul described fellow Christians as "fellow soldiers" (Phil. 2:25; Philem. 1:2). On another, he wrote, "Join with me in suffering, like a good soldier of Christ Jesus. No one serving as a soldier gets entangled in civilian affairs, but rather tries to please his commanding officer" (2 Tim. 2:3-4). Likewise, Peter instructed his readers to "arm yourselves" with a willingness to suffer like Jesus did (1 Pet. 4:1). Paul encouraged Timothy to "keep your head in all situations, endure hardship, do the work of an evangelist, discharge all the duties of your ministry," just as he himself had "fought the good fight," finished the race, and kept the faith (2 Tim. 4:5-7). In what is likely the most famous New Testament military metaphor, Paul instructed Christians to ready themselves for battle with the devil by putting on "the full armor of God," including the "belt of truth," "breastplate of righteousness," boots of readiness, "shield of faith," "helmet of salvation," and "sword of the Spirit, which is the word of God" (Eph. 6:10-17).[48] "As servants of God," he wrote, we equip ourselves "with weapons of righteousness in the right hand and in the left" (2 Cor. 6:4-7). "So let us put aside the deeds of darkness and put on the armor of light" (Rom. 13:12). We must "fight the battle well" and "fight the good fight of the faith … until the appearing of our Lord Jesus Christ" (1 Tim. 1:18; 6:12-14).

Note that although these passages compare the Christian mission to soldiering, none of them do so in a way that communicates anything positive about soldiering or violence in general. They all praise wholly nonviolent attributes, none of which are unique to soldiering but most of which are best *analogized* in soldiers: complete devotion to a commanding officer, a willingness to sacrifice and suffer for a cause greater than oneself, execution of duty regardless of the cost, self-discipline, endurance, faithfulness, equipping yourself for (spiritual) battle, etc.[49]

In reality, all the New Testament's military metaphors tell Christians to be *like* soldiers in their nonviolent attributes (e.g., their singleness of purpose, their disciplined pursuit of such, and their willingness to suffer and sacrifice to achieve it) but *unlike* soldiers in their violent attributes (e.g., by telling them to wage war with nonviolent weapons like truth, righteousness, preparedness, faith, and salvation instead of with violent weapons like swords, spears, and arrows).

These metaphors encourage Christians to wage war, but to do so only with nonviolent weapons. That's their whole point: fight like typical soldiers, but don't use the same weapons as typical soldiers. For as Paul declared, "though we live in the world, we do not wage war as the world does. The weapons we fight with are not the weapons of the world" (2 Cor. 10:3-4). This is because we fight a different type of enemy: "For our struggle is not against flesh and blood, but against the rulers, against the authorities, against the powers of this dark world and against the spiritual forces of evil in the heavenly realms" (Eph. 6:12).

To state it more directly, the military metaphors don't compare Christians to soldiers in every way. Instead, they compare them in some ways and contrast them in others. That's what metaphors do— they compare *non-identical* things. We must keep the differences intact. We must not lose sight of which military characteristics are being promoted and which aren't. Just as the soldier encounters discussed in Chapter 3 only endorse what they actually say they endorse, the military metaphors only commend what they actually say they commend. And when we look carefully, we see that none of them commend violence. Instead, they contrast the physical weapons of violence with the spiritual weapons of nonviolence and call Christians to equip themselves with the latter, not the former.

To cite the New Testament's military metaphors as supporting the use of violence contradicts the very point they were employed to make. They employ warfare imagery to promote nonviolence, not violence. "Rightly understood," Hays writes, "these metaphors witness powerfully against violence as an expression of obedience to God in Christ." In them, "the warfare imagery is drafted into the service of the gospel, rather than the reverse."[50] Or as Guy Frank Hershberger warned, "The Christian warfare as described in the New Testament is of such a nature that one cannot use it as an argument for the military warfare of nations without doing great violence to the Scriptures."[51]

Parabolizing God's Eradication of Evil

The Bible's warfare worldview also helps explain the violence in Jesus's parables, a few of which are pretty brutal. Here's a sampling: an authority figure (usually a king, master, or landowner) throws evildoers into a blazing furnace, hands them over to jailers to be tortured, crushes them with rocks, cuts them to pieces, beats them with many blows, binds them and throws them into the darkness where there is weeping and gnashing of teeth, banishes them to the eternal fire prepared for the devil, and even has them killed in front of him.[52] As usual, however, we will find that such stories don't justify human violence or prove that Jesus wasn't a pacifist.

For one thing, parables are not intended to be interpreted literally in every respect. They are imaginative stories designed to teach a spiritual truth or moral lesson. They make their point "indirectly by the use of comparison, analogy, or the like."[53] They employ hypothetical scenarios with a mix of realistic and unrealistic details to make a central point. They claim God's kingdom is *like* X in *some* way, not that it is *identical* to X in *every* way. To read every detail in them as literally true is to misread them.

Jesus's parables aim to change hearts and minds, not to provide an encyclopedic description of reality. He designed them to shape behavior more than impart data. He intends for them to change the way we think and act, not fill us full of facts. They are fictitious stories employed to illustrate a kingdom-related precept or principle, not historical accounts of events that have happened or will happen exactly as described.

Each parable's moral lesson is located in its main storyline, not in its details. The details, some more realistic than others, exist to help make the primary point. In the oral culture of Jesus's day, it likely had to be this way. To be memorable, the overriding lesson had to be short, simple, and central. Consequently, not every detail conveys a central and vital meaning. Instead, most exist to support a predominant truth. "The only safe rule for interpreting the parables of Jesus," concludes Hershberger, "is to discover the point He wishes to make, and to remember that the details of the story have value only as they illustrate this point."[54]

In each of Jesus's violent parables, violence is always a supporting detail, not the lesson. It always emphasizes or reinforces some other primary point. Here are a few examples:

- In the Parable of the Unmerciful Servant, a king forgives the massive debt of one of his servants only to watch that servant refuse to forgive a tiny debt owed to him, so the king revokes his forgiveness and hands the servant "over to the jailers to be tortured, until he should pay back all he owed." Then Jesus proclaims, "This is how my heavenly Father will treat each of you unless you forgive your brother or sister from your heart." (Matt. 18:21-35)

- In the Parable of the Wise Servant, a master returns to his house to discover that the servant he had left in charge had abused his power by beating his fellow servants and drinking heavily, so the master "cut him to pieces and assign[ed] him a place with the hypocrites, where there will be weeping and gnashing of teeth." (Matt. 24:45-51)

- In the Parable of the Weeds, a landowner who has sown his field with wheat seeds discovers that an enemy has also sown it with weeds, so he tells his servants to "collect the weeds and tie them in bundles to be burned," which Jesus later explains (to his disciples after the crowd leaves) symbolizes his return to earth to "weed out of his kingdom everything that causes sin and all who do evil" and "throw them into the blazing furnace, where there will be weeping and gnashing of teeth." (Matt. 13:24-30, 36-43)

- In the Parable of the Wedding Banquet, a king notices an inappropriately clothed guest at his son's wedding feast and tells his servants to "tie him hand and foot, and throw him outside, into the darkness, where there will be weeping and gnashing of teeth." (Matt. 22:1-14)

- In the Parable of the Tenants, a landowner who had rented his vineyard to some farmers sent his servants to collect some of the harvest, but the farmers kept beating and killing them. Finally, the owner sent his son to collect, but they killed him too. "What then will the owner of the vineyard do?" asked Jesus. "He will come and kill those tenants and give the vineyard to others." (Mark 12:1-11)

- In the Parable of the Sheep and the Goats, Jesus is depicted, upon his return to earth, welcoming into his kingdom those who loved the needy and sending those who didn't "into the eternal fire prepared for the devil and his angels," where there is "eternal punishment." (Matt. 25:31-46)

Notice that the point of all these parables—which are representative of all of Jesus's violent parables—is to warn that whoever fails to do God's will, which is usually depicted as loving others, will be judged and thrown out of God's kingdom. In other words, they provide notice, in varying ways, that God will eventually judge and eradicate evil. The point is never to explain or exemplify the proper human use of violence. Anytime someone other than the authority figure (or someone acting under his direction) uses violence, their actions are condemned. And anytime the authority figure uses violence, it is always to discourage or expel unloving behavior (e.g., failing to take care of the poor, refusing to forgive, beating people, killing, etc.).

To state the point more generally, the authority figure always uses violence to encourage obedience to Jesus's commands. And, as we've already seen, his commands are wholly nonviolent. Therefore, to the extent the violent parables have something to say about the ethics of violence, they implicitly condemn it. By directly communicating God's hatred of sinful, unloving behavior, they indirectly communicate his hatred of violent behavior.

To tell stories with harsh and violent characters to encourage obedience to nonviolent commands is not to condone harsh and violent conduct. Precisely the opposite—much like the soldier metaphors, Jesus used a few parables employing violent analogies to make antiviolence points. In this way, Jesus's violent parables advocate nonviolence. Again, Jesus's purpose in telling these parables was to change his listener's behavior, to move them away from disobedience and toward love for God and neighbor.

Knowing Jesus's pedagogical objective also sheds light on why he often described God's victory over evil in terms of violence. Like a good teacher, he was meeting humanity where it was and communicating to it in language and analogies it understood. His first-century audience only knew of one type of victory: victory through superior violence. Jesus hadn't yet introduced the world to victory through self-sacrificial love. The Jews were still a persecuted minority to whom God had promised a Messiah who would conquer their enemies and reestablish his kingdom. The parables were, among other things, a means of affirming that promise and assuring them of God's ultimate success via the vocabulary that they, and the rest of the world, understood—the vocabulary of violence. So a few of Jesus's parables used violence to analogize victory, not only because doing so fit the Bible's warfare worldview, but also because it fit its audience's violent worldview.[55]

The parables were not literally detailing how God conquers evil. For starters, given the purpose and nature of parables, viewing every authority figure as a perfect representation of God would be going too far. To analyze every detail of each authority figure's behavior as a metaphysically accurate depiction of how God's judgment functions is to overanalyze it and go beyond the proper limits of the genre. Even in those parables in which the authority figure does represent God, they claim he is *like* God in *some* way, not that he is *identical* to God in *every* way.[56] Again, analogies compare *non-identical* things, and we must keep their differences intact. We must not interpret every detail of each authority figure's character or actions as reflective of God's true character or actions. The parables were designed not to convey such information, but to change behavior.

We shouldn't interpret the allegorical depictions of God or Jesus using violence any more literally than we interpret the other allegorical elements in these parables and the rest of the New Testament. They don't suggest that God employs violence any more than the New Testament analogies about his judgment coming "like a thief in the night" suggest he steals.[57] God is no more a conqueror who literally wields violence than he is a farmer who literally throws seeds, as in the Parable of the Sower.[58] These stories no more support the conclusion that God uses violence than they support the conclusion that we can buy or earn our way into eternal life, as in the Parables of the Hidden Treasure and the Pearl.[59] As far as these parables are concerned, God will no more use violence at the final judgment than he will commend dishonest business practices, as in the Parable of the Shrewd Manager.[60] Jesus didn't intend for us to interpret God's use of violence in these parables literally any more than he intended for us to literally buy a sword, literally hate our parents, literally cut off the body parts that cause us to sin, or literally drink his blood and eat his flesh.

The violent authority figures in Jesus's parables reveal that God hates evil and will eventually eradicate it, but they don't necessarily reveal *how* he will do so. They figuratively stress the importance of obedience (to Jesus's nonviolent commands!) and the very real consequences of disobedience, as well as provide hope to the oppressed (by reassuring them that God will eventually overthrow their oppressors, forever!). They attempt to persuade us to avoid evil, not explain how God's judgment operates on a metaphysical level or demonstrate that he directly, personally, and violently punishes evildoers.

Plus, if Jesus's life and death have anything to say about it (and they do), God conquers evil through self-sacrificial love, not violence. Why conclude that Jesus's analogical parables or Revelation's symbolic imagery provide a more accurate representation of how God fights and conquers evil than how God actually fought and conquered evil while on earth?

Nonetheless, even if we interpret everything about the parables literally, including the authority figure's use of violence to conquer evil, they still don't justify *human* violence. At most, all the violent parables describe *God, Jesus,* or *angels* using violence *during the final judgment.* Each one makes it abundantly clear that God is the one who does the judging and punishing.[61]

Even under the most pro-violence reading possible, the violent parables are *descriptions* of *God's* end-time actions, not *instructions* for *us* to follow. They don't point to the authority figure and say, "Do this." They say, "This is what *God's* final judgment will accomplish." They don't—in contrast to all the other numerous New Testament passages that instruct us to leave such things to God—order us to mimic the authority figure's judgment and punishment ourselves. They order us to obey Jesus's commands to love others so we will avoid such judgment and punishment. They include violence to provide allegorical ethical motivation *to be nonviolent*, not literal ethical instruction on how to properly be violent.

Jesus's first-century life remains our moral standard. His actual ethical instructions, like those in the Sermon on the Mount, remain our marching orders. The parables don't change this. They reinforce it. We are still called to obey and mimic the Jesus of the Gospels, not the allegorically violent God or Jesus of the end-time parables. We are to bear witness to God's loving kingdom, not his final judgment. We are to give the world a foretaste of heaven, not hell.

Maybe the ethics of the Sermon on the Mount don't apply to God's future judgment. Maybe they do. I don't know. What I do know is that (1) any violence God may use at the final judgment doesn't justify our use of violence today, and (2) God's use of violence in Scripture (whether he employs it directly or merely channels others' violence) is always antiviolence, always designed to eradicate human violence.[62]

Why the Bible Uses Warfare Terminology

The New Testament does not employ violent metaphors, analogies, and parables to condone violence. It employs them to communicate that an urgent, universal conflict of utmost importance is underway, one that God wants us to join him in and one that will require the same commitment, discipline, and self-sacrifice as waging a violent war.

When you need to convey ideas of this magnitude, particularly the seriousness of what's at stake, sports analogies simply won't do. This isn't a game. It is life and death. The fate of creation hangs in the balance.

The violent metaphors, analogies, and parables are also not meant to provide ethical guidance on the proper use of violence. They don't give us our marching orders. They give context to our marching orders. They don't detail our rules of engagement. They give meaning to our rules of engagement. They don't teach us *how* to fight evil. They reaffirm our calling *to* fight evil in the first place.

To determine how God wants us to fight evil, we must look to Jesus's actual ethical instructions. Jesus didn't always speak in analogies, metaphors, and parables. He did make direct propositional statements, and he did issue commands—see the Sermon on the Mount.

When we look to the Sermon on the Mount, and to Jesus's other ethical teachings, we clearly see that he wants us to fight nonviolently. His battle plan is simple: love. That's it. To wage war on evil as Jesus taught and did, we need only to serve others nonviolently. The war we are fighting, the war between God and Satan, is a war between love and unlove, nonviolence and violence.

As we move on to examining the book of Revelation in the next two chapters, keep what we've learned in this chapter in mind. It will come in handy.

---

[1] For general additional info on how prevalent the theme of spiritual warfare is throughout the entire Bible, see Richard Beck's *Reviving Old Scratch: Demons and the Devil for Doubters and the Disenchanted* (InterVarsity

Press, 2015), and for a more specific treatment, see also Chapters 21-24 ("The Principle of Cosmic Conflict") in Greg Boyd's *The Crucifixion of the Warrior God.*

[2] C. S. Lewis, "Christianity and Culture" in *Christian Reflections*, ed. Walter Hover (Grand Rapids: Eerdmans, 1967), 33.

[3] Deut. 10:17; Ps. 136:2-3; Dan. 2:47; Matt. 11:25; Luke 10:21; Acts 17:24. First Timothy 6:15 also refers to God as "the blessed and only Ruler, the King of kings and Lord of lords," and Revelation 15:3 calls him "King of the nations."

[4] Rev. 17:14; 19:11-16. In the Old Testament, "Lord" is often a translation for the Hebrew word *adon*, which means one possessed of absolute control or a master or a ruler of his subjects. In the New Testament, "Lord" is almost universally a translation for the Greek word *kurios*, which means master.

[5] Luke 10:19; Matt. 13:38; 1 John 5:19; John 17:15; Matt. 12:24; Mark 3:22; Luke 11:15.

[6] Eph. 6:11-12; Acts 26:17-18; Col. 1:12-13.

[7] John 12:31; 14:30; 16:11; 2 Cor. 4:4; Eph. 2:2.

[8] Matt. 4:8-10; Luke 4:5-8.

[9] Rev. 12:9, 17; 13:3-4, 7-8, 12, 14-17; 14:8; 17:2; 18:3, 23; 20:3, 7-8.

[10] Boyd, *The Crucifixion of the Warrior God*, 22579.

[11] 1 John 3:8; 2 Cor. 11:3.

[12] Rev. 12:9; 20:3.

[13] Matt. 13:36-43; Acts 5:3; 1 Chron. 21:1; 1 Cor. 7:5; Eph. 2:1-2; 1 John 3:8.

[14] 1 Pet. 2:11; Rom. 6:12; Gal. 4:3-9.

[15] 1 Thess. 2:18; 2 Cor. 12:7; Matt. 13:19; Mark 4:15; Luke 8:12; 2 Cor. 4:4.

[16] See generally Genesis, Job, and Revelation. For his courting of Jesus, see Matt. 4:1-10, Luke 4:5-8, and Mark 8:33.

[17] Richard Beck, *Reviving Old Scratch: Demons and the Devil for Doubters and the Disenchanted* (Fortress Press, 2016), 275, Kindle.

[18] Rev. 12:4; Matt. 2:13-16.

[19] Matt. 3:13-4:11; Luke 3:21-4:13; Mark 1:9-13.

[20] For example, see Mark 1:23-34; 3:9-11; 5:1-42; 7:24-30; Matt. 12:22-28; 15:22-28; Luke 4:31-39; 11:14-20; 13:10-13; Acts 10:37-38.

[21] John 13:2, 27; Luke 22:2-4.

[22] Dietrich Bonhoeffer, *The Cost of Discipleship* (Touchstone, 2012), 1836, Kindle.

[23] 1 John 3:8; John 12:31; 16:11; Heb. 2:14.

[24] Jesus's miracles demonstrate this, as do all of his symbolic statements about the inherent natures of the two kingdoms: one life-giving, and the other life-taking.

[25] Frank Viola, *Insurgence: Reclaiming the Gospel of the Kingdom* (Baker Books, 2018), 475, Kindle.

[26] In the Bible, the expressions "kingdom of God" and "kingdom of heaven" refer to the same thing. We know this for several reasons: (1) the different Gospel writers use them both to describe the same sayings of Jesus; (2) Matthew himself uses them interchangeably in 19:23-24; and (3) the Gospel writer who used the expression "kingdom of heaven" almost exclusively (Matthew) was writing to the Jews, many of whom used "heaven" as a circumlocution for "God" out of respect for the commandment in Exodus 20:7 to "not misuse the name of the Lord your God."

[27] Luke 4:43; 8:1; 16:16; Matt. 4:23; 9:35; 24:14.

[28] As Ronald J. Sider notes, "There is almost universal agreement among New Testament scholars today that the core of Jesus's proclamation was the 'gospel of the kingdom.'" See *Just Politics: A Guide for Christian Engagement* (Brazos Press, 2012), 1106, Kindle. Hauerwas concurs with Sider's assessment: "there is widespread agreement that one of the most significant 'discoveries' of recent scholarship is that Jesus's teaching was not first of all focused on his own status but on the proclamation of the kingdom of God." See *The Peaceable Kingdom: A Primer in Christian Ethics* (Notre Dame, IN: University of Notre Dame Press, 1991), 73.

[29] Matt. 5:1-12, 19-20; 7:21; 11:11; 18:1-5; 21:31-32, 43; Mark 10:15; Luke 7:28; 18:17; John 3:3-5.

[30] Acts 1:1-3.

[31] John Howard Yoder, *The War of the Lamb: The Ethics of Nonviolence and Peacemaking*, ed. Glen Stassen, Mark Thiessen Nation, and Matt Hamsher (Brazos Press, 2009), 607, Kindle.

[32] Lee C. Camp, *Mere Discipleship: Radical Christianity in a Rebellious World* 2nd Edition (Brazos Press, 2008), 1637, Kindle.

[33] The New Testament says the cross was the means by which God demonstrated his love for us, forgave our sins, atoned for our sins, redeemed us, reconciled us to himself and others, made us righteous, gave us eternal life, defeated evil, and freed us from slavery to sin. See Rom. 3:24-25; 5:8-11, 15-19; 6:6-7; 8:1-3; John 1:29; 3:16; Eph. 1:7-8; 2:14-16; 5:1-2, 25; Gal. 2:20-21; 3:13-14; 6:14; Col 1:19-22; 2:13–15; 1 John 4:10; 1 Pet. 1:18-19; 2:24-25; 3:18; 1 Cor. 15:3; 2 Cor. 5:14-21; 13:4; Heb. 2:14-15; 9:28.

[34] To learn more about this aspect of what Jesus was doing on and through the cross, check out the Christus Victor theory of the atonement.

[35] Col. 2:15; Heb. 2:14-15.

[36] See also Rev. 17:14; 19:16.

[37] N. T. Wright, *How God Became King: The Forgotten Story of the Gospels* (HarperOne, 2012), 792, Kindle.

[38] Ibid., 792 and 2798.

[39] Ibid., 792 and734.

[40] Ibid., 2738.

[41] N. T. Wright, *Simply Jesus: A New Vision of Who He Was, What He Did, and Why He Matters* (HarperCollins, 2011), 2562, Kindle.

[42] To explain it another way, an awareness of the different kingdom periods resolves the Bible's seemingly contradictory use of near, present, and future tenses to describe its timing and presence.

[43] Matt. 13:36-43, 25:31-46; 2 Pet. 3:10-13; 1 Cor. 15:24-26; Rom. 16:20; Rev. 11:15; 20:10, 14.

[44] Rev. 21:4.

[45] Rev. 12:12.

[46] C. S. Lewis, *Mere Christianity*, 46.

[47] Charles H. Spurgeon, *Devotional Classics of C. H. Spurgeon: Morning & Evening I & II*, Volume I of *The Fifty Greatest Christian Classics* (Lafayette, IN: Sovereign Grace Publishers, Inc., 1990), 209.

[48] See also 1 Thess. 5:8.

[49] In addition to the verses cited above, see also the relatively well-known analogy in Luke 14:31.

[50] Hays, *The Moral Vision of the New Testament*, 9268.

[51] Guy Franklin Hershberger, *War, Peace, and Nonresistance* 5th Edition (Scottdale, PA: Herald Press, 2009), 306-307.

[52] Matt. 13:38-42, 49-50; 18:32-35; 21:42-44; 22:1-14; 24:45-51; 25:30; 25:41-43; Luke 12:46-47; 19:27; 20:9-18.

[53] www.dictionary.com

[54] Hershberger, *War, Peace, and Nonresistance*, 305.

[55] Similarly, the use of graphic imagery made the parables more memorable, which was important in the oral tradition of Jesus's audience.

[56] The parables usually start with "The kingdom of God is like a king who...." That's different than starting with "God is like a king who...." At a minimum, such wording indicates that we aren't supposed to assume God is exactly like the king in the story.

[57] 1 Thess. 5:2; Matt. 24:42-44.

[58] Matt. 13:3-9, 18-23.

[59] Matt. 14:44-46.

[60] Luke 16:1-13.

[61] Matt. 13:24-30, 36-43, 47-50; 18:21-35; 21:33-46; 22:1-14; 24:45-51; 25:14-46; Mark 12:1-12; Luke 12:42-48; 14:15-24; 16:19-31; 19:11-27; 20:9-18.

[62] Yes, even God's use of violence in the Old Testament was antiviolence. See my book *The Old Testament Case for Nonviolence.*

CHAPTER 6

REVELATION PART I: SETTING THE SCENE

The book of Revelation is infamously violent, easily the most violent book in the New Testament and arguably the most violent book in the entire Bible. Within its pages, people are subjected to plagues and earthquakes, made to drink blood, inflicted with festering sores, poisoned by polluted water, tortured by mutant locusts, tormented with burning sulfur, burned alive, starved to death, dashed to pieces like pottery, crushed by collapsing buildings, flattened by hundred-pound hailstones, gored by wild beasts, eaten by birds, and forced to kill each other. Even children are struck dead. If it was a movie, Revelation would be a horror film.

Most troubling of all, much of the book's violence is attributed—often indirectly, but occasionally directly—to God or Jesus. No wonder Nietzsche described it as "the most rabid outburst of vindictiveness in all recorded history"[1] and Martin Luther claimed he could "in no way detect that the Holy Spirit produced it."[2]

Not helping the situation, Revelation is notoriously difficult to interpret. Throughout Christian history, theologians of all persuasions have acknowledged its complexities and struggled to make sense of its strange, obscure, and elaborate imagery. Many Christians and non-Christians alike view it as the most puzzling part of the most puzzling book ever compiled. Respected intellectuals have called it everything from "a curious record of the visions of a drug addict"[3] to "a book of riddles that requires a revelation to explain."[4]

These two traits—Revelation's seemingly God-sanctioned carnage and its interpretive impenetrability—combine to create a dangerous text. Indeed, throughout history, few pieces of literature have been read with such disastrous results. Christians themselves have frequently weaponized the book, citing it to justify horrendous acts of violence against believers and non-believers alike.[5]

At a minimum, for most Christians, Revelation is the trump card that disproves Jesus's pacifism and demonstrates the salvific, redemptive nature of violence. It's what ultimately confirms their belief that nonviolence is generally a good thing but not always obligatory, not even for Jesus, and that ultimately only violence can defeat evil.

In a sense, it's hard to blame them. On its face, Revelation does seem to negate the pacifistic Jesus of the Gospels. Instead of continuing to depict a Savior who conquers evil through self-sacrificial love (à la the cross), it appears to portray a Savior who must eventually use violence to finish the job by fighting a "war to end all wars."

Nonetheless, as we are about to see, it is possible to make sense of the book of Revelation, and to do so in a way that confirms Jesus's pacifism and reiterates the nonviolent ethics he taught. In fact, when read within its proper framework, it's a beautifully subversive, deeply antiviolence book.

Granted, Revelation's complexity—with its comingling of genres, its ubiquitous and arcane symbolism, its intertextual nature, and its hodgepodge of worldly and otherworldly phenomena—leaves the door open to a plethora of interpretations. But that doesn't mean all such interpretations are equal. They aren't. Some are demonstrably more reasonable than others, while a not-insignificant number lend credence to G. K. Chesterton's quip that although Revelation's author "saw many strange monsters in his vision, he saw no creature so wild as one of his own commentators."[6]

As with most difficult biblical passages, Revelation forces its reader to make big, important interpretive choices. It presents enough textual proof to support many mutually exclusive readings and makes the reader choose among them. In our case, Revelation can be read violently or nonviolently. Should you desire it, its pages contain enough evidence to support a violent reading. But if you see the wisdom in a nonviolent reading, its pages contain just as much (and, I believe, more) evidence to support that as well.

Regrettably, the nonviolent reading is less popular because it requires two ingredients not possessed by everyone: First, the reader must be open to reading it nonviolently. I can't offer much help here. If you're not willing to even consider a nonviolent reading, and many people aren't, then nothing I can say will suffice.

Second, the reader must willingly put forth the work necessary to read Revelation in context. You will not encounter the nonviolent interpretation via a surface level, literalistic analysis. To see Revelation's antiviolence message, you must go deeper. You must expend the effort to understand its biblical, literary, and historical contexts. That's what the rest of this chapter and the next are about. In what follows, we will examine three key pieces of context and then explore the primary antiviolence symbols and themes that arise out of them.

The Apocalyptic Genre

The first step to properly interpreting any writing is identifying and understanding its literary genre. We need to know whether we are reading poetry, journalism, science fiction, or academic history because we interpret them differently. For instance, no one reads the poetic Psalms the same way they read Paul's rhetorical argumentation in his letter to the Romans, and neither of them are read in the same manner as the gospel narratives. To do so, to approach them with the same expectations and perspectives, would be foolish.

The same is true for Revelation, but doubly so. Most misinterpretations of it, particularly those that turn it into a dangerous text, are rooted in a fundamental misunderstanding of its literary form and purpose.

Unfortunately, Revelation doesn't fit neatly into a single genre. It is a hybrid of multiple literary forms, including letter, apocalypse, prophecy, and liturgy. Nonetheless, it does clearly have a dominant genre: apocalypse. It begins by proclaiming itself to be "The revelation of Jesus Christ," wherein "revelation" is the English form of the Greek word *apokalypsis*.[7] Therefore, to properly interpret Revelation, we need to understand a bit about apocalyptic writing as it was used by the biblical writers and throughout the ancient Near East.

When most people today hear the word *apocalypse*, they think of a world-ending cataclysmic event, usually involving violent natural disasters like earthquakes, tsunamis, or asteroid showers. But in Greek, the word means "an unveiling." It means to reveal, to uncover, to unmask. Biblical apocalyptic writing is, as N.T. Wright describes, "the sudden unveiling of a previously hidden truth."[8] The author has been allowed to see things others haven't, to see aspects of reality that aren't readily apparent, and he desires to pass them on. This is the purpose of Revelation. Wright explains:

> John, its author … is picking up a way of writing well known in the Jewish world of the time. This way of writing was designed to correspond to, and make available, the visions and 'revelations' seen by holy, prayerful people who were wrestling with the question of the divine purpose. Like the theatre audience, they and the rest of God's people felt themselves in the dark. As they studied their ancient scriptures and said their prayers, they believed that the music was building up to something, but nobody was quite sure what. But then, like someone all by themselves in the theatre for the first performance, the 'seer'—the word reflects the reality, 'one who sees' something that other people do not—finds that the curtain is suddenly pulled up. Suddenly the 'seer' is witnessing a scene, is in fact invited to be part of a scene, within God's ongoing drama.[9]

Similarly, apocalyptic writing is prophetic, but not in the modern sense of the word. It is prophetic in the biblical sense, which is less about predicting the future and more about explaining the present, less about foretelling future reality and more about truthfully describing current reality. It unmasks what is really going on, how the fallen world really works—not merely how it will be at some future point. Prophecy, in the biblical tradition, intends to provide insight into today as much as foresight about tomorrow. It is as much about the human historical experience here and now as it is about history written in advance.

Combining these two aspects of Revelation—the apocalyptic (in the Greek sense) and the prophetic (in the biblical sense)—allows us to understand the book as the unveiling of present reality from God's perspective. It is, in other words, the unveiling of true reality. Hence the book opens by proclaiming itself to be a recording of what God has revealed to its author, John, who in Chapter 4 of Revelation describes how he was taken up to God's throne room to view the unfolding of everything else described in its remaining eighteen chapters.[10]

Of course, Revelation has something to say about the future. There is a predictive aspect to it. But it is not, contrary to popular evangelical opinion, a codebook of end-time events just waiting to be properly deciphered.

To begin with, its predictions aren't hidden. Apocalyptic writing in the biblical tradition employs symbolism to *uncover* how reality works, not *encode* future events. It intends to *reveal*, not *conceal*. Revelation's predictions need not be hidden because they aren't about specific details or events. Instead, they are about general, big-picture consequences and happenings. Revelation predicts things like (1) what life on earth will continue to be like as long as humans persist in embodying Satan's kingdom instead of God's (i.e., as long as they continue living violently instead of lovingly),[11] and (2) God's eventual, total, and final defeat of evil and injustice and the complete reestablishment of his kingdom on earth.

The wildly creative, otherworldly, fantasy-laden, over-the-top characters and scenes Revelation employs to make such broad prophecies were not intended to provide a historically accurate chronicling of actual events that must occur before such things will come to pass, let alone supply a realistic description of how each will literally unfold. Rather, they were, in keeping with the apocalyptic genre and the oral culture of the day, designed for dramatic appeal, memorability, and symbolic communication. Revelation is not a puzzle to be solved by identifying which symbols represent which historical figures and events, but "a visionary theological and poetic representation of the spiritual environment within which the church perennially finds itself living and struggling," to borrow Hays' description.[12]

Revelation's use of symbolism cannot be overemphasized. Apocalyptic literature communicates almost entirely, if not entirely, through symbolism. It speaks through pictures, not logic. It appeals to the imagination, not rational deduction. It aims to influence its hearers by providing them with an imaginative experience, not by filling them full of facts. It employs graphic, emotionally charged symbols in order to awake and arouse, not to impart academically accurate data. It is theatrical, not scientific.

Here's the most important thing about symbolism, both in general and in Revelation: By definition, it isn't meant to be interpreted literally. Something is symbolic when it is figurative, representative, illustrative, emblematic, or allegorical. In other words, something is symbolic precisely when and because it is *not* literal. Thus, Revelation employs symbolism precisely so it will *not* be read literally as an imparting of encyclopedic facts about how God will eradicate evil, when the world will end, etc. Jesus himself set the tone for a nonliteral interpretation of Revelation when, during his instructions to its author in the first chapter, he explained that the seven golden lampstands and seven stars were *symbols* for the seven churches and their seven angels.[13]

Symbolism seeks to express the invisible or immaterial through visible representation. Symbols are employed to communicate intangible literal truths, not to depict literal beings or events. As such, Revelation's symbolism is meant to be interpreted truthfully, but not literally. Its word pictures aim to give visible representation to theological truths, not provide a literal depiction of theological characters and events.

For example, Jesus is not literally a lamb. He isn't covered in wool and doesn't walk around on four legs while chewing grass and saying "baaa." But he is vulnerable and nonviolent like a lamb. And he was sacrificially slaughtered like one.

Likewise, the 144,000 virgins with God's name written on their head who are said to have never told a lie aren't literally 144,000 individuals who have tattooed their faces, never had sex, and never been untruthful. It is a symbolic number representing a large number (which derives from 12 x 12 x 1,000, being the number of Israel's tribes squared and then multiplied by Revelation's number of magnitude and power), of God's faithful followers—those who have clung to the truth and not defiled themselves with idolatry, which is often symbolized in the Bible as adultery or sexual promiscuity.

Similarly, Revelation's use of "millennium" and "thousand years" isn't intended to denote a literal period of one thousand calendar years but instead symbolically denotes a long, indefinite time period. At least, that's what it meant to the Jewish people and other biblical writers. When the Psalmist wrote that God owns the cattle on a thousand hills, he wasn't claiming that God's ownership of cattle is limited to *only* one thousand hills.[14] And when he declared that one day in God's courts is better than a thousand elsewhere, he wasn't claiming that 1,001 days elsewhere would be better than one day in God's courts.[15]

In fact, if we interpret all of Revelation's symbols literally, the book would end in Chapter 6. There, we see described the sun turning black, the moon turning blood red, the stars falling to earth, the heavens receding like a scroll being rolled up, and every mountain and island being dislodged.[16] If all of that literally occurred, life on earth would cease to exist. But the story, along with human life, goes on. The stars even magically reappear in the sky in Chapters 8 and 12, only to be partially destroyed again each time.[17] As this single example demonstrates, applying a literal lens to all of Revelation's visionary imagery produces logical absurdities and contradictions.

Selective literal interpretations won't do either. In many ways, they are worse. They betray the interpreter's self-interested agenda, revealing his presuppositions through what he does and doesn't want to be literal. Here's what Brian Zahnd says on the subject:

> If some people admit that the lamb with seven horns and seven eyes is obviously symbolic but insist that Jesus riding a flying white horse is literal, they're going to have to explain their system of interpretation. Or if they claim that Jesus is going to wage a literal war upon his return but the sword depicted as proceeding from his mouth is symbolic, again they're going to have to justify the logic of their system.[18]

In one of his recorded sermons, Pastor Bill Johnson highlighted the hypocrisy of interpreting some of Revelation's symbols literally but not others.[19] During a discussion of the passage in Revelation 20 that describes the dragon being bound with chains and cast into a bottomless pit for a thousand years, he had the following conversation with his audience, who at the time believed in a literal millennium:

Bill: The Dragon, literal or figurative? Is it a real dragon?

Audience: Figurative.

Bill: The chains, literal or figurative? Is it actual chains?

Audience: Figurative.

Bill: The bottomless pit, literal or figurative?

Audience: Figurative.

Bill: The millennium, literal or figurative?

Audience: (stunned silence)

We could go on, but you get the point. "The only way to consistently interpret the book of Revelation," Zahnd concludes, "is to acknowledge that *everything* is communicated by symbol."[20] To interpret Revelation's visionary imagery literally is to misinterpret it.

Doing so not only violates the genre but causes one logical problem after another. To interpret it correctly, we must acknowledge its symbolic nature and fix our eyes on the literal truths it communicates, not treat it as a codebook of literal end-time characters, events, and timelines.

John's original audience would have intuitively understood all of this. While many of its symbols are mysterious to us two thousand years after its writing, they would have been familiar to those who shared John's cultural, political, historical, and religious context. As Hays puts it, they "would have read such symbolism 'as fluently as any modern reader of the daily papers reads the conventional symbols of a political cartoon.'"[21] To be more precise, they would have noticed and understood its symbolism as effortlessly as "American readers of a political cartoon featuring an elephant and a donkey immediately know that the elephant symbolizes the Republican party and that the donkey symbolizes the Democrats."[22]

We must never forget that Revelation was written by a first-century author to a first-century audience to address first-century problems using first-century literary devices and images.[23]

The Warfare Worldview on Steroids

The second piece of context necessary to properly interpret the violence in Revelation is the Bible's warfare worldview, which the previous chapter explained in detail. Revelation takes it to the next level. It is the most explicit, most graphic description of God's ongoing war with Satan in all of Scripture. It is cosmic theater on a grand scale, depicting God engaged in an epic, universal, all-important, very real, life-and-death struggle for sovereignty over the world. The entire book is about how God's kingdom (through Jesus and his followers) has been, is, and will continue taking back territory (and the pain, setbacks, and difficulties associated with such an endeavor) until it conquers all. It is the climax of the clash between good and evil, phrased in terms of the Lamb versus the Beast, angels versus demons, Christians versus earthly empires, and New Jerusalem versus Babylon.

Here is Revelation's main narrative: God's kingdom fights, suffers, and eventually triumphs over Satan's. This, Michael J. Gorman explains, is what apocalyptic writing is all about:

Apocalyptic literature gives expression to apocalyptic theology. At the core of this kind of theology is a *cosmic* dualism, the belief that there are two opposing forces at work in the universe, one for evil (usually Satan and his demons) and one for good (usually God and the angels). This cosmic dualism gets embodied in real-life struggles between good and evil on earth, resulting in a more *historical* dualism of conflict between the children of God or light and the children of Satan or darkness.[24]

But just like all of the other violent imagery in the New Testament, Revelation's imagery is metaphorical and analogical. Yes, it is the great cosmic conflict on steroids, but they are symbolic steroids. Its warfare imagery is not meant to be interpreted literally. It isn't even the main point. It is used illustratively, as a means of making some other, more primary point. More specifically, it employs violent warfare imagery not to condone physical violence or human warfare (or teach us some other ethical lesson about how to properly use violence for good) but to communicate that an urgent, universal conflict of utmost importance is underway, one that God wants us to join him in and one that will require the same commitment, discipline, and self-sacrifice as waging violent war. We must not let the means of communication—the heavily symbolic and highly dramatic apocalyptic genre—distract us from the message that is truly being communicated.

So yes, Revelation declares that we are engaged in battle. Yes, it is a call to arms and a command to conquer. But it does not call us to a physical battle or to violent action. It calls us to fight a more important war, a spiritual war, and to fight it by remaining faithful to the way of Jesus—not by wielding earthly power. In fact, it commands us to fight evil by *refraining* from violence. It implores us to *resist* the allure of violent warfare. Yes, it uses militaristic language, but it does so in an anti-militaristic way, just like Paul's soldiering metaphors and Jesus's violent parables.[25] This will become evident as our analysis proceeds.

By the way, to say that we must interpret Revelation's violent imagery within the context of the Bible's larger warfare worldview is simply to say that we must interpret it within the context of the rest of Scripture. Proper exegesis demands it. As a subset of the Bible, Revelation must be read and understood through the lens of the rest of the Bible, not vice versa. We must filter what it says about God and Jesus through what we already know about them as revealed in the rest of the Canon, particularly the Gospels.

The Audience and Their Problem

Another key to properly interpreting any writing is understanding its intended audience and purpose. To whom was it written and why?

Authored by a first-century Christian living in political exile, Revelation was written to address the political crisis faced by the early church, which was a minority group struggling with how to remain faithful to Jesus's kingship while living amid a competing empire. Roman society was pressuring the early Christians to conform and compromise. It was telling them to be good Roman citizens, to acquiesce to the supremacy of the nation. It was urging them to fall in line like everyone else, to support the empire's systems of power and domination (through everyday loyalty, and occasional contributions of time and money) and to participate in its growing emperor cult (through taking part in its rituals and festivals designed to promote the worship of Caesar).

Do these things, said Rome, or suffer the consequences. Become productive, contributing members of the Roman Empire and enjoy the relative safety, comfort, and control it provides or remain faithful to the subversive, anti-power kingship of Jesus and suffer the social, economic, and political repercussions. Go through the patriotic motions and live a normal life or resist such idolatry and endure constant civil discomfort and occasional public mistreatment— maybe even death. In short, compromise and avoid persecution, or remain faithful and suffer it. This was the early church's quandary.

Look at what Revelation says to the seven churches. While each receives a message tailored to its own unique situation, the overarching issue is always about remaining faithful and avoiding compromise. The churches in Ephesus, Pergamum, Thyatira, and Philadelphia are all praised for persevering and enduring hardship and abuse, while the church in Smyrna is encouraged to remain faithful during its impending persecution.[26] Three of those churches—Ephesus, Pergamum, and Thyatira—are also chastised for their acts of unfaithfulness, from forsaking love to accepting false teachings that lead to idolatry.[27] The church in Sardis is generally criticized for not holding fast to God's teachings, while those few members who have held true are applauded.[28] The church in Laodicea is not praised for anything but is instead condemned for accumulating wealth to become self-sufficient, just like empires do.[29]

When we read these messages to the seven churches, Gorman observes, "we are struck by two major problems that the churches are confronting: the reality of various kinds of persecution, and the strong temptation to accommodate, with accommodation perhaps being seen by some as the way to avoid or stop persecution."[30]

The sheer amount of discussion about faithfulness in Revelation is overwhelming once you know to look for it. John sets the tone from the start: beyond identifying himself as a servant of God, the only other thing he says about himself is that he is someone who has patiently endured suffering for God's kingdom.[31] And in addition to the faithfulness-centered messages to the churches at the beginning of Revelation, further calls for faithfulness and patient endurance occur throughout the book.[32] Numerous times, God's followers are even explicitly commanded to remain faithful *unto death*, and are then praised for doing so.[33] Similarly, the faithful are repeatedly promised rewards while the unfaithful are repeatedly warned of judgment.[34]

It's easy to see how empire fits into this faithfulness equation. We need only ask ourselves, "Who is doing the persecuting, and why?" Who: the Roman Empire. Why: because the church is refusing to grant it supremacy.

Throughout Revelation, empire is God's enemy. The whole book is one big battle between his kingdom and earthly kingdoms, and its entire narrative portrays empire as Satan's primary tool, the predominant means by which he effectuates his earthly reign and opposes God's kingdom and its followers. Numerous times, John explicitly states that earthly rulers are under Satan's deceptive and seductive control and influence.[35] They receive their power from him, they worship him, and they are used by him to wage war on God's people.[36] Empire is, according to Revelation, public enemy number one.

What Revelation says about the two beasts and Babylon bears this out. Let's start with the beasts. The first half of Revelation talks a lot about God's kingdom conquering, but it doesn't specify who or what needs to be conquered. At the midway point, in Chapters 12 and 13, we get our answer: the evil trinity, which comprises the dragon (Satan) and his two underling beasts. For numerous reasons, almost all biblical scholars agree that the first beast, the one from the sea, represents the Roman Empire specifically and imperial power more generally.[37] Similarly, the second beast, the one from the earth, symbolizes the supporters and promoters of imperial power, from high-level government officials to local elites and lowly bureaucrats. The description of the second beast's actions in 13:11-17 makes this clear. So the first beast is empire and the second its minions.

Now consider what Revelation says about the beasts. "The dragon gave the beast his power and his throne and great authority.... The whole world was filled with wonder and followed the beast. People worshiped ... the beast and asked, 'Who is like the beast? Who can wage war against it?'" (13:2-4). "[The beast] opened its mouth to blaspheme God, and to slander his name and his dwelling place and those who live in heaven. It was given power to wage war against God's holy people and to conquer them. And it was given authority over every tribe, people, language and nation" (13:6-7). The beast sent forth demonic spirits to perform signs and "go out to the kings of the whole world, to gather them for the battle on the great day of God Almighty" (16:13-14). "The beast and the kings of the earth and their armies gathered together to wage war against the rider on the horse and his army" (19:19). They joined forces to "wage war against the Lamb" but Jesus will "triumph over them" (17:14). Ultimately, "the beast was captured" and "thrown alive into the fiery lake of burning sulfur" where he "will be tormented day and night for ever and ever" (19:19-20; 20:10). Then those who "had not worshiped the beast or its image and had not received its mark on their foreheads or their hands ... came to life and reigned with Christ a thousand years" (20:4). As you can see, the beast (earthly empire) and God's kingdom (including Jesus and his followers) don't much care for each other.

What Revelation says about Babylon sends the same message. Specifically, Babylon symbolizes the city of Rome.[38] More generally, it represents the fruit of empire, a great city of wealth and power built upon the violent control, domination, and exploitation of others. (When John first sees Babylon in 17:3-5, it is riding the first beast.) Babylon is, according to the symbolism of Revelation, the center and epitome of Satan's kingdom and his violent means of ruling.

No wonder Revelation says such harsh things about it. It calls Babylon "the great mother of prostitutes and of the abominations of the earth" and "the great prostitute who corrupted the earth by her adulteries" (17:5; 19:2). "With her the kings of the earth committed adultery, and the inhabitants of the earth were intoxicated with the wine of her adulteries" (17:2).[39] "The merchants of the earth grew rich from her excessive luxuries" (18:3). She gave herself "glory and luxury" and boasted of her power (18:7). She became "drunk with the blood of God's holy people, the blood of those who bore testimony to Jesus" (17:6; 18:24). God's followers are explicitly called to "come out of her, my people, so that you will not share in her sins, so that you will not receive any of her plagues" (18:4). When Babylon is defeated, those who mourn are "the kings of the earth who committed adultery with her and shared her luxury" and "the merchants of the earth" who amassed wealth under her reign (18:9-19). Those who rejoice are God's people, particularly those that were slaughtered by her, and they rejoice alongside the heavenly assembly.[40] Babylon, the center and epitome of empire, is, to put it mildly, no friend of God's. It misleads, oppresses, and destroys his creation.

These anti-empire themes, so blatantly revealed in the beasts and Babylon, permeate Revelation. Throughout the book, the behavior of empire is continually contrasted with faithfulness to God. Repeatedly, the ways of empire are associated with evil, sin, and disobedience. The whole book declares the entire system of empire—its politics, its economics, its religion, etc.—to be of Satan and directly in conflict with God's kingdom and Jesus's kingship.

The two kingdoms are incompatible. Allegiance to empire is antithetical to allegiance to God; the worship of Caesar precludes the worship of God; and trust in imperial power is at odds with trust in God.

We cannot serve two masters or enlist in competing armies. We must decide whose way of living and ruling we will adopt and cultivate, whose version of reality we will embrace and embody. Will it be the power politics of earthly governments, or the servant kingship of Jesus? Will we align ourselves with the world's rulers who excel at violently imposing their will on others, or with the slaughtered lamb who self-sacrificially loves others even unto death?

We must choose between the civil religion of empire and discipleship in Christ.

According to Revelation, empire is an idol, a competitor god. Empire demands that we worship it, while God insists that we worship him alone.[41] Empire calls us to acknowledge its supreme rule, while God declares Jesus to be the world's rightful ruler.[42] Empire claims that it is in control and will win, while God assures us of his own control and inevitable victory.[43] God even declares that those who remain faithful to him, those who avoid complicity with earthly nations, will someday be given authority to rule over those same nations.[44]

As you've likely noticed by now, Revelation paints earthly rulers in a much different light than some other New Testament passages. There is no hint of government being God's servant for humanity's good; humble submission to it is nowhere encouraged; and honor is the last thing it is due. Revelation leaves no room for compromise or complacency. What it demands instead is an ethic of opposition. "Revelation is above all else a political resistance document," writes Hays. "It refuses to acknowledge the legitimacy and authority of earthly rulers and looks defiantly to the future, when all things will be subjected to the authority of God."[45]

Revelation reflects the reality that human government usually, if not always, oversteps its limited God-ordained role and asserts itself as a savior—as the provider, protector, and hope of the world, not to mention the driver of history. This is why the book is, as Gorman observed, "a sustained stripping of the sacred from secular power—military, political, economic—and a parallel sustained recognition of God and the Lamb as the rightful bearers of sacred claims, the only worthy recipients of divine accolades."[46]

Again, the issue Revelation addresses is not when or how the world will end, but how Christians should react to the temptations of earthly power. Does God really want us to refrain from participating in the secular religion of safety, comfort, and control, particularly at the cost of persecution, or can we make some seemingly harmless compromises to avoid seemingly unnecessary suffering? Does strict faithfulness really matter? Does it make a difference? Does it contribute to God's victory? Or are Christians wasting their lives by following the crucified Christ instead of the world's power brokers, who appear to be in control? This was the dilemma facing the first-century church.

Revelation provides a clear and emphatic answer to these questions: Don't compromise! Not even one iota! Remain faithful, even when it seems ineffective! And if necessary, hold steady even unto death! By doing so, you are taking back territory for God. You are helping Jesus rule the world. You are defeating Satan and his minions. Be assured, God is in control and this is how he has chosen to restore creation—through you, through your faithful embodiment of his radically nonviolent kingdom, as exemplified by his pacifistic, self-sacrificial, crucified Son.

In this sense, Revelation encourages faithfulness in two ways: by comforting the afflicted and afflicting the comfortable.[47] The faithful who were suffering persecution needed reassurance that God was in control, encouragement to remain steadfast, and hope that it was all worth it. On the other hand, those who were getting too cozy with empire needed to be warned of the negative consequences of doing so and challenged to repent and correct course.

This explains Revelation's frequent and severe warnings about God's judgment and ultimate victory. Those warnings accomplish both purposes: by sending the message that God hates, judges, and will eventually eradicate injustice, they offer hope to those suffering under empire's oppression and caution to those flirting with it, and rouse those already sharing its bed. The more frequently and graphically Revelation conveys and communicates this message of God's justice, the more effectively it accomplishes those aims.

This also explains Revelation's recurring promises of eternal rewards for the faithful. They provide encouragement, motivation, and hope by reassuring God's followers that their suffering is temporary, that death doesn't have the final word, that God will eventually restore all creation to its original state of harmony, and that the faithful will partake in that harmony, forever. Although Revelation is known more for its diatribes against injustice and unfaithfulness, it talks almost as much about the rewards for doing justice and remaining faithful. For those who believe in and yearn for God's justice, it is an immensely hopeful book.

Revelation's motivational message—remain faithful and reap the rewards or compromise and suffer the consequences—is good news for some and sobering news for others. Either way, however, it's all about promoting faithfulness.

This is what biblical prophecy does. It speaks words of comfort and challenge to God's people. As such, Revelation's "visions of the future," notes Gorman, "are not an end in themselves but rather a means—both to warn and to comfort."[48]

Leave it to us comfortable Westerners residing in—and dutifully supporting—the largest, most powerful government the world has ever seen to ignore (or worse, misappropriate) Revelation's words of comfort, assume its words of challenge apply to everyone but ourselves, and read the book not as a critique of empire, violence, and complacency but as a puzzle book of literal, end-time actors and events designed for our decoding entertainment.

Now that we've set Revelation's context (its genre, warfare worldview, audience, and intended purpose), let's explore its primary antiviolence themes and symbols.

---

[1] Friedrich Nietzsche, *The Birth of Tragedy and the Genealogy of Morals*, trans. Francis Golffing (Garden City, NY: Doubleday, 1956 [1887]), 185.

[2] Michael J. Gorman, *Reading Revelation Responsibly: Uncivil Worship and Witness Following the Lamb Into the New Creation* (Eugene, OR: Cascade Books, 2011), 1.

[3] George Bernard Shaw, as quoted in Preston Sprinkle's *Fight: A Christian Case for Non-Violence* (David C. Cook, 2013), 2589, Kindle.

[4] Thomas Paine, as quoted in Michael J. Gorman's *Reading Revelation Responsibly: Uncivil Worship and Witness Following the Lamb Into the New Creation* (Cascade Books, 2011), 198, Kindle.

[5] For example, according to Wes Howard-Brook and Anthony Gwyther, Revelation "has been used and abused to support a wide variety of social movements, from the modern-day Branch Davidians incinerated at Waco and the Heaven's Gate community ... to the second-century Montanists and the thirteenth-century Apostolic Brethren." They also claim that its "underlying schema of history inspired, consciously or unconsciously, Hitler's notion of the Third Reich and Karl Marx's dream of the revolution of the proletariat." See *Unveiling Empire: Reading Revelation Then and Now* (Orbis Books, 1999), 607, Kindle.

[6] G. K. Chesterton, *Orthodoxy*, Centennial Edition (Nashville: Sam Torode Book Arts, 2009), 13.

[7] Rev. 1:1.

[8] N. T. Wright, *Revelation for Everyone* (Westminster John Knox Press, 2011), 146, Kindle.

[9] Ibid.

[10] Rev. 1:1-2, 10-11; 4:1-2.

[11] Or as Zack Hunt describes it, "The [biblical] prophets weren't fortune-tellers. They were warning the people of God about what would happen in the future if they did or didn't act a certain way in the present. Which is why biblical prophecy is about the present as much as or more than it is about the future." In other words, "Revelation isn't a road map to the future. It's a model for how to live in the present.... This is, after all, why John's apocalypse begins with letters to churches in the present, with instructions on how to live in the here and now." See *Unraptured: How End Times Theology Gets it Wrong* (Herald Press, 2019), 2114 and 2320, Kindle.

[12] Hays, *The Moral Vision of the New Testament*, 4872.

[13] Rev. 1:20.

[14] Ps. 50:10.

[15] Ps. 84:10.

[16] Rev. 6:12-14.

[17] Rev. 8:12; 12:4.

[18] Brian Zahnd, *Sinners in the Hands of a Loving God: The Scandalous Truth of the Very Good News* (WaterBrook, 2017), 2063, Kindle.

[19] Bill Johnson, "Mission Possible," CD. 15:30 minute mark to 17:05 minute mark.

[20] Zahnd, *Sinners in the Hands of a Loving God*, 2063.

[21] Hays, *The Moral Vision of the New Testament*, 4848 (citing G. B. Caird 1956, *Principalities and Powers*, Oxford: Clarendon, 6).

[22] Ibid., 4849.

[23] This is not my description but a paraphrase of a point Gorman made in *Reading Revelation Responsibly*. See Kindle location 1703.

[24] Gorman, *Reading Revelation Responsibly*, 480.

[25] As this chapter has already demonstrated and will continue doing so, Revelation has much in common with the violent metaphors, analogies, and parables discussed in the prior chapter—it is symbolic and not intended literally, it aims to change behavior rather than impart facts, its moral lessons are found within its main narrative rather than its symbolic details, etc. Likewise, the violence in Revelation no more justifies human violence today than the violent metaphors, analogies, or parables do, and neither proves that Jesus was not a pacifist.

[26] Rev. 2:2-3, 10, 13, 19, 24; 3:8, 10.

[27] Rev. 2:4, 14-15, 20.

28 Rev. 3:1-4.

29 Rev. 3:17.

30 Gorman, *Reading Revelation Responsibly*, 1904.

31 Rev. 1:9.

32 Rev. 1:3; 2:26; 6:9-11; 12:17; 13:10; 14:3-5, 12; 16:15; 17:14.

33 Rev. 2:10; 12:11; 13:10; 14:13; 20:4, 6.

34 Rev. 1:3; 2:4-5, 7, 11, 16-17, 26-28; 3:3-5, 10, 12, 21; 7:14-17; 11:18; 14:7, 9-11, 13; 16:1-21; 19:9; 20:4-6, 12-13; 21:3-8; 22:1-5; 22:7, 12, 14.

35 Rev. 13:3-4, 14; 18:3, 23; 20:2-3, 7-10.

36 Rev. 11:7; 13:2-4, 7, 8, 12; 16:5-6, 13-14, 16; 17:12-14; 19:19; 20:7-9.

37 For example, in 17:9-14, John explains that the first beast's seven heads symbolize seven kings (five that are fallen, one that is, and one that is yet to come) and its ten horns symbolize an additional ten kings (who have yet to receive a kingdom).

38 As N.T. Wright bluntly states in his book *Revelation for Everyone*, "Anyone who knows anything about the book of Revelation knows that 'Babylon' is used as a symbol later in the book … where John without a shadow of doubt means 'Rome.'" See Kindle location 2272.

39 See also 14:8.

40 Rev. 18:20, 24; 19:1-8.

41 Rev. 13:8, 12, 15-17; 14:9-11; 16:1-2, 10-11; 20:14-15; 21:8.

42 Rev. 1:4-5; 2:26-27; 3:14; 11:15; 12:5; 17:14; 19:15-16.

43 Rev. 15:3-4; 21:24-27; 16:19; 17:12-14; 18:4-8, 21; 19:1-2, 15, 19-21; 20:10.

44 Rev. 2:26-27; 5:9-10; 20:4, 6; 22:5.

45 Hays, *The Moral Vision of the New Testament*, 4803.

46 Gorman, *Reading Revelation Responsibly*, 1195.

47 This description is a paraphrase of a point Hays made in *The Moral Vision of the New Testament*. See Kindle location 4977.

48 Gorman, *Reading Revelation Responsibly*, 581.

CHAPTER 7

REVELATION PART II: ANALYZING ITS VIOLENCE

In the first scene of John's vision, we find ourselves in God's heavenly throne room, where he is surrounded by various heavenly attendants (elders, angels, and creatures) and is holding a scroll sealed with seven seals (5:1). When an angel asks who is worthy to break the seals and open it, no one is found in heaven or on earth who qualifies, causing John to weep (vv. 3-4). Inside the scroll is God's redemptive plan for human history, how he intends to save the world from evil (i.e., Satan's reign) and restore it to its originally created state of peace, joy, and harmony—and it appears doomed to remain locked. But then an elder says to John, "Do not weep! See, the Lion of the tribe of Judah, the Root of David, has triumphed. He is able to open the scroll and its seven seals" (v. 5). At once, John sees "a Lamb, looking as if it had been slain, standing at the center of the throne" (v. 6). The creatures and elders begin worshipping the Lamb, singing, "You are worthy to take the scroll and to open its seals, because you were slain, and with your blood you purchased for God persons from every tribe and language and people and nation" (v.9). Then thousands of angels surround the throne and begin proclaiming, "Worthy is the Lamb, who was slain, to receive power and wealth and wisdom and strength and honor and glory and praise!" (v. 12). After that, the scene shifts as we watch the Lamb open each seal.

Most biblical scholars agree that this scene is the central and centering vision of the entire book, the interpretive key to everything else in it, including all the strange visions that follow. This is as it should be. The declaration that the slaughtered lamb (who is obviously Jesus!) is alone worthy to open the scrolls places him at center stage, right where he belongs. His sacrificial death on the cross is the center point of the entire Bible, the event around which everything else revolves.

John also stresses Jesus's primacy in numerous other ways throughout Revelation. He begins the book by declaring it to be a revelation from and about Jesus.[1] He claims that Jesus, along with God, is the source of salvation[2] and declares him to be "the First and the Last," the "Living One" who holds "the keys of death and Hades" (1:5, 17-18). Jesus is, in fact, depicted opening each of the seven seals, thereby unleashing God's judgment on evil, his final victory over Satan, and the reestablishment of his eternal kingdom on earth as it is in heaven. Such a sequence culminates in John proclaiming, "The kingdom of the world has become the kingdom of our Lord and of his Messiah, and he will reign for ever and ever" (11:15). At other points in the book, Jesus battles, defeats, and is declared ruler over the beast and his army of earthly kings.[3] When Babylon is defeated, a voice declares "the wedding of the *Lamb* has come" (19:7). John calls God's restored creation, the New Jerusalem, "the wife of the *Lamb*," a city whose foundation is "the twelve apostles of the *Lamb*" (21:9, 14). And only those whose names are written in the "*Lamb's* book of life" are allowed into it (21:27). Likewise, when Eden is restored at the end of Revelation, God's throne is referred to as "the throne of God and of the *Lamb*" (22:1, 3). John even defines God's followers as those who remain faithful to Jesus, follow him wherever he goes, and conquer as he conquers.[4] The evidence goes on, but you get the point: Jesus is key.

Notice the nonviolence implications of this opening scene. At the heart of God's salvation plan, the key to unlocking the meaning and purpose and aim of human history, is not a slaughtering lion but a slaughtered lamb. The elder introduces the one who "has triumphed" as "the Lion of the tribe of Judah," but when John looks he sees "a Lamb, looking as if it had been slain" (5:5-6). Shockingly, the Messiah, the central character in all of history, turns out not to be a lion but a harmless, defenseless, nonviolent lamb—and a slain one at that. N.T. Wright calls this "one of the most decisive moments in all scripture. What John has *heard* is the announcement of the lion. What he then *sees* is the lamb."[5] Similarly, Eugene Boring labels it "one of the most mind-wrenching and theologically pregnant transformations of imagery in literature."[6] After this symbolic redefinition, John never again refers to God's great conqueror as a lion—only a lamb.

This surprise echoes the surprise of the Gospels. They say, "Surprise! The anticipated militaristic messiah is actually a vulnerable pacifist!" Revelation says, "Surprise! The conquering lion is actually a slaughtered lamb!"

Furthermore, this scene declares Jesus's nonviolent self-sacrifice essential to his ability to open the scrolls. Notice why both the elders and angels proclaim him worthy to do so: "You are worthy to take the scroll and to open its seals, *because you were slain*," and "Worthy is the Lamb, *who was slain*." So not only is the lowly servant Jesus key, which is shocking in itself, but he is key *because* he was slain! To put it in terms of violence, Jesus possessed the ability to unlock God's plan because he lovingly absorbed violence, not because he wielded it in a more just way.

This whole scene is a direct assault on the notion of redemptive violence. It confirms the gospel message that God conquers through uncompromising, nonviolent, self-sacrificial love, not through a superior ability to wield force. Violence does not redeem or save; Christlike love does. Violence is not the most powerful force in the universe; Christlike love is.

All of this affirms my earlier point that Revelation, particularly what it says about Jesus, must be read through the lens of the Gospels, not vice versa. The Gospels present a historical account of the real-life Jesus—of how he lived, what he taught, and how he conquered evil. Revelation simply presents a symbolic, dreamlike vision of Jesus. Interpreting more obscure, more symbolic passages through clearer, more literal passages is fundamental to proper literary interpretation. Therefore, we must interpret Jesus's symbolic actions in Revelation through his literal actions in the Gospels—not vice versa.

Revelation's first two verses set the reader up to do precisely this. By declaring itself to be the revelation of and from Jesus, the book orients the reader toward what she already knows about Jesus from his actual life. Plus, as Hays points out, "The image of the triumphant 'Lamb that was slaughtered' is unintelligible apart from the Gospel narratives of Jesus's crucifixion and resurrection."[7] So is Revelation's claim that Jesus has *already* triumphed (3:21; 5:5), which only makes sense if the reader already knows Jesus's life story.

When we interpret Revelation from this proper perspective, it becomes clear that Jesus's actions in Revelation, even those that are widely believed to be undeniably violent, are entirely consistent with his nonviolent actions in the Gospels. Let's take a look.

Jesus Waging War on a White Horse

We begin with Revelation's most famous depiction of a supposedly violent Jesus. Here's the passage:

> I saw heaven standing open and there before me was a white horse, whose rider is called Faithful and True. With justice he judges and wages war. His eyes are like blazing fire, and on his head are many crowns. He has a name written on him that no one knows but he himself. He is dressed in a robe dipped in blood, and his name is the Word of God. The armies of heaven were following him, riding on white horses and dressed in fine linen, white and clean. Coming out of his mouth is a sharp sword with which to strike down the nations. "He will rule them with an iron scepter." He treads the winepress of the fury of the wrath of God Almighty. On his robe and on his thigh he has this name written: king of kings and lord of lords.
>
> And I saw an angel standing in the sun, who cried in a loud voice to all the birds flying in midair, "Come, gather together for the great supper of God, so that you may eat the flesh of kings, generals, and the mighty, of horses and their riders, and the flesh of all people, free and slave, great and small."
>
> Then I saw the beast and the kings of the earth and their armies gathered together to wage war against the rider on the horse and his army. But the beast was captured, and with it the false prophet who had performed the signs on its behalf. With these signs he had deluded those who had received the mark of the beast and worshiped its image. The two of them were thrown alive into the fiery lake of burning sulfur. The rest were killed with the sword coming out of the mouth of the rider on the horse, and all the birds gorged themselves on their flesh. (Rev. 19:11-21)

Interpreted literally, there's no doubt Jesus commits violence in this passage. But John didn't intend for this passage to be interpreted literally. Like the rest of his vision, everything in it is symbolic.

For starters, notice that Jesus's robe is bloody prior to his battle with the beast and kings. Given that he hasn't yet engaged the enemy and considering what we already know about Jesus from the Gospels (e.g., he only ever shed his own blood) and from his first appearance in John's vision (as an already slaughtered lamb), we should conclude the blood on Jesus's robe is his own, not that of his enemies.

This interpretation is consistent with all the other bloodshed in Revelation. Anytime shed blood is mentioned, it is always the blood of Jesus or his followers. With one possible exception, which we will analyze soon, Revelation never refers to blood that has been shed by God, Jesus, or their followers. As Preston Sprinkle notes, "God never causes His enemies to bleed in Revelation—literally or symbolically."[8] On the other hand, God's enemies cause his followers to bleed so thoroughly they are described as being drunk on blood.[9]

The fact that Jesus's heavenly army is "dressed in fine linen, white and clean" (v. 14) also indicates the blood on Jesus's robe is his own, not that of his enemies. As John has previously explained, the "fine linen stands for the righteous acts of God's holy people" (v. 8) and white robes represent those who "have washed their robes and made them white in the blood of the Lamb" (7:14). Indeed, white robes had already been given to "those who had been slain because of the word of God and the testimony they had maintained" (6:9-11). So according to Revelation itself, even Jesus's troops ride into battle having already been in contact with *his* blood and having already mimicked his *self*-sacrifice. Like Jesus, they engage the enemy with righteous acts, not with violent weapons, and they overcome by self-sacrificially shedding their own blood, not by making others bleed. As the voice from heaven puts it, they triumph "by the blood of the Lamb and by the word of their testimony" (12:11).

From this perspective, not only is the blood on Jesus's robe his own blood, but it symbolizes two important things about him, and consequently about his followers: it indicates he has *already* conquered via the cross, and it represents *how* he has conquered (and continues to conquer)—through the self-sacrificial shedding of his own blood. Revelation, not to mention the rest of the New Testament, makes these points over and over again in various ways. Sometimes Revelation even makes them simultaneously, like when it declares that Jesus "has freed us from our sins by his blood" (1:5) or proclaims that by his blood he "purchased for God persons from every tribe and language and people and nation" (5:9).

So yes, there's a lot of blood in Revelation, but it all flows from Jesus and his followers, not their enemies. And yes, the means by which Jesus and his followers conquer often involves the shedding of blood, but it's always their own blood. Therefore, when read through the lens of the Gospels and in the context of everything Revelation claims, the symbolic nature of the blood on Jesus's robe is clear: it is his own, not his enemies'.

Now consider the sword Jesus wields in this passage. Curiously, it comes out of his mouth. In fact, every time John depicts Jesus with a sword in Revelation, it is always protruding from his mouth.[10]

But why? What is John trying to communicate with such a placement? Why depict it coming out of his mouth instead of held in his hand?

Because John wants us to know the sword is symbolic, not literal. It's a metaphor. It represents something other than a literal sword. Had John wanted it to represent a literal sword, he would have, among other things, placed it in Jesus's hand.

This isn't the first time in Scripture we encounter a metaphorical sword associated with someone's mouth. On many occasions, the Psalmist referred to men whose tongues and words were sharp as swords.[11] Isaiah claimed that God had made his "mouth like a sharpened sword" (Isa. 49:2). He also prophesied that Jesus "will strike the earth with the rod of his mouth; with the breath of his lips he will slay the wicked" (Isa. 11:4). Even Jesus himself spoke of metaphorical swords: "Do not suppose that I have come to bring peace to the earth. I did not come to bring peace, but a sword" (Matt. 10:34).

The sword is not a sword. It's a symbol. Jesus no more literally wields a sword than he is literally a lamb with seven horns. Jesus is a man, not a lamb. And he wields a cross, not a sword.

So the sword is a symbol, but what does it symbolize? Generally, it symbolizes powerful speech. The sword signifies power, and its protrusion from the mouth signifies speech. In this specific situation, because the sword is coming out of *Jesus's* mouth, it symbolizes speaking God's truth. It has nothing to do with violence. It's about proclaiming the truth of and about God.

As if to remove any doubt about the symbolic nature and meaning of the sword, two verses before John mentions it, he declares that the name of the person whose mouth it protrudes from is "the Word of God" (v. 13). John isn't the only biblical writer to metaphorically correlate the Word of God with a sword. Here's the author of Hebrews: "For the word of God is alive and active. Sharper than any double-edged sword, it penetrates even to dividing soul and spirit, joints and marrow; it judges the thoughts and attitudes of the heart" (Heb. 4:12). And here's Paul: "Take the helmet of salvation and the sword of the Spirit, which is the word of God" (Eph. 6:17).

John sprinkled additional circumstantial evidence of this symbolic meaning throughout Revelation. For example, when we first meet Jesus in 1:16, he is holding seven stars representing the messengers of seven churches and has a sharp sword coming out of his mouth. He shows up on the scene equipped with a message of truth, not with weapons of violence. Similarly, in his instructions to the church of Pergamum, Jesus warns it to turn away from *false* teachers or he will "fight against them with the sword *of my mouth*" (2:14-16). He counters false teaching with truth telling.

Given that the heart of the biblical conflict between God and Satan centers on truth versus deceit, it makes sense that Jesus fights with the truth. This theme—God's truth versus Satan's deceit—goes all the way back to the Garden of Eden, where the serpent deceived Adam and Eve into believing that God's instructions were not for their good, and it continues all the way through Revelation.

In fact, this theme plays a prominent role in Revelation. God and Jesus are repeatedly referred to as truthful, as are their followers and those whom they allow into their kingdom. On the other hand, their adversaries include: a *false* prophet; a beast who is primarily described as a blasphemer and deceiver; the whorish Babylon, who is accused of leading the nations astray; and Satan, whose primary crime against humanity is deceiving it and who is eventually thrown into the Abyss to keep him from doing exactly that.[12] And remember, the whole point of the book of *Revelation* is to *reveal* the truth. Its title is the Greek word *apokalypsis*, which means an unveiling of truth. This is what biblical prophecy is all about, and it is why John's vision centers around him being given access to the heavenly control room. There, he is shown reality for what it truly is, in stark contrast to the deceptive view Satan perpetuates on earth.

So whose view of reality will you adopt? Satan's claim that violence-based earthly dominion is supremely powerful and effective or God's claim that Christlike love is? What weapon will you wield in your pursuit of good—redemptive violence or redemptive love?

At this point, you may be thinking, "Okay, you've convinced me that the bloody robe and protruding sword don't symbolize a violent Jesus, but what about all the other violence-related talk in this passage, like the reference to Jesus waging war, striking down the nations, ruling with an iron scepter, treading the winepress of God's wrath, throwing the beast and his cohorts into the fiery lake, and killing people with his mouth sword?" Good question. I'm glad you asked, because this is where things get really interesting.

The key to properly interpreting all the symbolism in this passage—and consequently, the key to realizing that none of its violence-related talk is intended to depict a violent Jesus—is understanding that John is simultaneously communicating two messages: (1) Jesus is at war, is powerful, and is a conqueror and (2) *how* Jesus wages war, exerts power, and conquers. Hence his seemingly contradictory mix of violent and nonviolent symbols. Let's take a quick look at how this dichotomy plays out.

First, in keeping with the biblical warfare worldview, John depicts Jesus at war with evil. This is no game. The struggle is real and the fate of the universe is at stake. So Jesus mounts a war horse, grabs his sword, gathers his army, and meets the enemy on the battlefield.

Second, Jesus hates injustice and intends to defeat it once and for all. He does not join the fight to become a martyr. He is in it to win it. He wields a sword to "strike down the nations" and aims to "rule them with an iron scepter." Earthly power brokers have defiled God's harmonious kingdom with injustice, and Jesus is livid: "He treads the winepress of the fury of the wrath of God Almighty."

Third, Jesus accomplishes his mission. He is victorious. He captures the beast and false prophet and throws them into the lake of fire. Then he uses his sword to kill the unjust kings of the earth and their armies.

These violence-related symbols exist to communicate that Jesus hates injustice, is at war with it, and will conquer it. Given the suffering God's followers were enduring, John is reassuring them that Jesus's seemingly ineffective way of fighting evil with nonviolent self-sacrificial love is not only effective but so powerful it will eventually eradicate evil. The entire book of Revelation is nothing less than an apocalyptic confirmation of exactly that.

In other words, the "striking down" and "killing" in this passage symbolize Jesus's victory and evil's defeat, not literal violence. After all, the nations that are destroyed in this passage reappear alive and well in numerous passages later.[13] So when John writes, "the rest were killed with the sword coming out of the mouth of the rider on the horse," he intends to communicate that Jesus conquers through truth, not that he literally kills people with a magic sword protruding from his mouth. Yes, Jesus will triumph over the unjust nations, he will defeat the beast and his minions, and he will vanquish those who persist in unloving behavior—but he won't do so with violence.

In short, the literal element of these violence-related depictions of Jesus is that he fights and conquers, not *how* he does so. These images demonstrate the existence of Jesus's power, not the type of power he possesses. They portray the fact of his victory, not his means of victory.

To determine *how* Jesus fights and defeats evil, we must look to the other symbolic details in this passage (and interpret them through the lens of the Gospels). We've already done this with Jesus's robe dipped in blood *prior to battle*, the sword *coming out of his mouth*, and his being named the *Word* of God, all of which symbolize nonviolent means. There's one more detail worth mentioning.

Although the passage describes Jesus riding out to wage war and the beast and kings of the earth gathering to oppose him, no actual battle is described. John moves directly from describing both parties readying themselves for battle to declaring that the beast and false prophets have been captured and disposed of, along with their followers (vv. 19-21). Jesus's final battle with evil turns out to be not much of a battle at all.[14]

So why doesn't John see or describe a battle? Because the battle has already been fought and won via Jesus's life, death, and resurrection![15] In Eller's words, "Jesus did the fighting on Good Friday; God confirmed the victory on Easter."[16] There's no need for another battle. John need not depict Jesus shedding his enemies' blood because Jesus has already struck the fatal blow by shedding his own blood.

The only thing left to do is for Jesus (and his followers) to bear witness to his already-won victory, a victory that was achieved entirely through nonviolent, self-sacrificial love. This is why Jesus is only armed with a sword coming out of his mouth. To finish off his enemy, he need only speak the truth about what he has already accomplished. He need only remain "Faithful and True," which is what John calls the rider on the white horse (v. 11).

John doesn't describe a battle because he knows that the true enemy, deceit, can't be overcome with physical fighting—only with truth. As Paul put it, "we do not wage war as the world does" and our weapons "are not the weapons of the world" because "our struggle is not against flesh and blood, but against the rulers, against the authorities, against the powers of this dark world and against the spiritual forces of evil in the heavenly realms" (2 Cor. 10:3-4; Eph. 6:12). Consequently, we employ non-physical weapons like "the belt of truth … the breastplate of righteousness … the shield of faith … the helmet of salvation and the sword of the Spirit, which is the word of God" (Eph. 6:14-17). Unlike physical weapons, such things "have divine power to demolish strongholds" by destroying "every pretension that sets itself up against the knowledge of God" (2 Cor. 10:4–5).

Jesus knew this. He knew that deceit is the primary poison and truth is the only antidote, which is why he embodied truth instead of employing violence in the Gospels. It's also why Revelation repeatedly portrays Jesus with a weapon that symbolizes truth (a sword coming out of his mouth) and why it declares that God's followers "triumphed over [Satan] ... by the word of their testimony" (12:11), not by wielding violence in more just and effective ways. Just as God spoke the universe into existence, he will, in a way, speak evil out of existence. That's the only way to do it. Physical fighting is futile.

Here's another reason John doesn't describe a battle: This passage is primarily about communicating *that* Jesus conquers, not *how* he conquers. How Jesus conquers was already well-known by John's audience. They knew all about the scandalously nonviolent, slaughtered lamb. So John is writing not to re-explain Jesus's ethics but to assure his readers that Jesus's seemingly powerless ethics are, in reality, supremely powerful.

To summarize, the key to realizing that none of the violence-related talk in this passage, or anywhere else in Revelation, is intended to depict a violent Jesus is separating the symbols that demonstrate the fact that Jesus is at war, is powerful, and is a conqueror from the symbols that demonstrate *how* he wages war, exerts power, and conquers. Jesus's riding a war horse, wielding a sword, ruling with an iron scepter, treading the winepress of God's wrath, striking down the nations, killing with his mouth sword, and throwing the beast into the fiery lake all symbolize his very real battle with and victory over evil. Jesus's robe being bloodied before battle, the sword being placed in his mouth, his name being the Word of God, and the absence of a physical battle all symbolize the *means* by which he wages war against and triumphs over evil.

In terms of symbolically depicting a nonviolent victory over evil, you could do much worse than this scene. Consider how difficult it is to portray nonviolent fighting and conquering. Even with the recent development of nonviolent tactics of resistance and numerous contemporary examples of successful nonviolent campaigns (e.g., Gandhi and Martin Luther King, Jr.), our fallen minds still equate fighting and conquering with violence. To wage war, to do battle, and to defeat the enemy is to use violence. To not use violence is, in most people's minds, to do nothing. All of this would have been even truer of John's first-century audience.

But if Jesus really does fight and conquer evil, then that fighting and conquering has to be depicted somehow. And if Jesus also really does fight and conquer nonviolently, then his fighting and conquering also has to be depicted in a way that doesn't betray his nonviolence.

This scene resolves the dilemma quite nicely by drawing the perfect balance between symbolizing a literal victory and symbolizing the counterintuitively nonviolent means of that victory. Sure, the symbols of victory are arguably more prominent than the symbols of means, but that's because the book's primary aim was to reassure the early Christians of God's power and control. Despite how dominant and unconquerable earthly power (in the form of Rome) appeared, they needed to be reminded that God's counterintuitive way of ruling (as demonstrated by Jesus) has won, is winning, and will win. So John's symbolic vision stresses the victory over its means, but it also includes enough means-related details to affirm what his readers already knew about Jesus's nonviolent modus operandi. Can you think of a better way to symbolically and metaphorically depict Jesus's nonviolent victory over his violent enemies than to portray him "killing" them with a sword *from his mouth*?

We must continually fight the fallen urge to selectively interpret all of Revelation's nonviolent images metaphorically and all of its violent images literally. When John writes, "the rest were killed with the sword coming out of the mouth of the rider on the horse" (19:21), it's contradictory to conclude that the killing is literal but the sword is figurative. They are both figurative.

Nothing in John's vision is literal. Just as Satan isn't literally a dragon, Babylon isn't literally a prostitute for hire, and a seven-headed beast won't literally emerge from the sea to kill Christians, Jesus isn't literally a seven-eyed lamb, doesn't literally tread a winepress owned by God, and won't literally regurgitate a sword while riding a flying horse.

Everything in John's vision is communicated symbolically. Instead of mentioning Jesus's death on a cross, John symbolizes it in a slaughtered lamb. Likewise, instead of explaining how Jesus fought evil when he walked the earth, John symbolizes it by clothing him in a robe dipped in his own blood and placing a sword in his mouth.

What's true about Revelation's symbols is the immaterial message they are trying to communicate, not the material representation they employ to do so. Jesus isn't truly a lamb, but he is truly like one in his harmlessness, his nonviolence, and his vulnerability. He doesn't truly wage violent war—he doesn't truly grab a sword, mount a horse, and kill people—but he does truly fight and defeat injustice. We must not lose sight of the distinction between literal truth and symbolic truth.

Before we move on to looking at two other passages popularly believed to portray a violent end-times Jesus, I want to point out one more massive advantage of this nonviolent interpretation of Jesus waging war on a white horse: it is consistent with everything else the New Testament, including Revelation, says about how Jesus behaved and taught his followers to behave. Three quick examples should suffice.

First, it is consistent with Revelation's own description of Jesus as a triumphant lion *and* a slaughtered lamb. In the sense we've been discussing them, they are not incompatible. On the contrary, they are both indispensable. Jesus fights evil with the ferocity and power of a lion, but his means of fighting resemble the nonviolent, vulnerable tactics of a lamb. He fights valiantly but not violently.

Second, it is consistent with how Revelation depicts God's followers conquering evil. We will explore what the book demands of Christians in more detail soon, but here's the gist: "They triumphed over him by the blood of the Lamb and by the word of their testimony" (12:11).

Lastly, and most importantly, it is consistent with how Jesus fought and conquered evil in the Gospels and on the cross. As demonstrated in previous chapters, his life, teachings, and death were all entirely nonviolent. He bore nonviolent witness to the truth of self-sacrificial love. He did not coerce, control, or kill.

Interpreting this passage, or any passage in Revelation, as a depiction of a violent Jesus subverts everything he said and did in the Gospels. When Jesus returns, he will not abandon his uniqueness and become just another Caesar. As Brian D. McLaren has written, the Jesus that walked the earth was not "a fake-me-out Jesus pretending to be a peace-and-love guy, when really he was planning to come back and act like a proper Caesar, more of a slash-and-burn guy, brutal, willing to torture, and determined to conquer with crushing violence."[17] Jesus isn't going to admit that his first trip to earth failed, that his crucifixion and resurrection were insufficient, that love doesn't always win, and that what is really needed is superior violence. He will not acknowledge that, as his critics have said all along, pacifism is naïve, passive, cowardly, hypocritical, ineffective, and irresponsible. Nor will he replace his "unrealistic" nonviolent commands with more "realistic" just war principles. "Those who live by the sword will die by the sword" will not become "those who live by a more just sword will reign with me in eternity." Jesus won't recant what he taught about loving your enemies, turning the other cheek, and repaying evil with good. He will not redirect his followers to lay down their crosses and take up their machine guns. Instead, Jesus's second coming will be consistent with his first, pacifistic one.

Revelation does not present a sudden, last-minute reversal of Jesus's nonviolent tactics. It represents a symbolic demonstration of the real-life power and effects of such tactics.

Likewise, Revelation is not a surprise overturning of the clear biblical trend away from violence and toward nonviolence, a trend I've discussed elsewhere.[18] Instead, it's a symbolic affirmation of it. Zahnd elaborates:

> The saddest thing is that the adherents of this schizophrenic Jesus often seem to prefer the violent Jesus over the peaceable Jesus. At a basic level they essentially see the Bible like this: After a long

trajectory away from the divine violence of the Old Testament culminating in Jesus renouncing violence and calling his followers to love their enemies, the Bible in its final pages abandons a vision of peace and nonviolence as ultimately unworkable and closes with the most vicious portrayal of divine violence in all of Scripture. In this reading of Revelation, the way of peace and love that Jesus preached during his life and endorsed in his death is rejected for the worn-out way of war and violence. When we literalize the militant images of Revelation we arrive at this conclusion: in the end even Jesus gives up on love and resorts to violence. Tragically, those who refuse to embrace the way of peace taught by Jesus use the symbolic war of Revelation 19 to silence the Sermon on the Mount.[19]

Again, we must interpret Revelation's symbolic Jesus through the lens of the Gospel's historical Jesus, not vice versa. John's visionary Jesus must not be allowed to contradict every other New Testament writer's real-life Jesus. A few obscure images in the Bible's most perplexing book do not trump "The Word [who] became flesh and made his dwelling among us" (John 1:14).

With this interpretive framework in mind, let's briefly look at two more passages in Revelation that are often cited as depicting a violent Jesus.

The Four Horsemen of the Apocalypse

When Jesus opens the first four seals, each unleashes a rider on a horse who wreaks havoc on humanity (6:1-8). The first rides a white horse, holds a bow, and gallops "out as a conqueror bent on conquest" (v. 2).[20] Rider two sits atop a fiery red horse, wields a large sword, and has the "power to take peace from the earth and to make people kill each other" (v. 4). The third rides a black horse, holds a pair of scales, and sows economic exploitation (vv. 5-6). Rider four has a pale horse, is named Death, and possesses the power to kill a fourth of the earth by sword, famine, plague, and wild beast (v. 8). When Jesus opens the sixth seal, a great earthquake occurs, causing everyone to hide from "the wrath of the Lamb" (vv. 12-16).

There's no doubt that violence results from Jesus's opening of the seals. But Jesus does not employ that violence, either directly or indirectly. He *allows* it, as the passive language ("was given") used throughout these verses indicates. Permit me to explain.

God's plan for redeeming all creation involves allowing Satan to show his true colors and humankind's disobedience to run its natural course, one riddled with violence and destruction. In opening these scrolls, Jesus is revealing what the world is like under Satan's reign and man's rebellion. He is shouting, "Look! This is the type of existence Satan's way of life produces!"

This is a natural stage in fallen humanity's moral evolution. Before it will choose God's way, humanity first must be permitted to arrogantly go its own way and experience the bitter fruit of doing so. It must be allowed to suffer the painful failure of trying to achieve peace, harmony, and salvation through its own means and power, through violence. It must be given the opportunity to realize that it has a problem and is helpless to fix it. Before it will go to the doctor for help, humanity must first realize it has a fatal disease and cannot cure it alone. Before it will voluntarily embrace a savior, humanity must be made aware of its need for a savior.

This is how a non-coercive God persuades. He doesn't force anyone to obey him. He allows us to exercise our free will in rebellious ways and then suffer the negative consequences—while he simultaneously demonstrates the positive consequences of obedience through those communities who embody his way of life. And all along, he sends prophets to continually highlight the differences between the two approaches. This is how an always-loving God convinces humanity that his way, the way of uncompromising self-sacrificial love, is best for all creation.

In this passage, Jesus is not inflicting punishment or causing destruction. He's revealing the self-punishing, self-destructive effects of humanity's violence. By unleashing the violent riders, Jesus no more causes the violence they commit than parents cause the violence their children commit when they unleash them into the world through procreation.

Trampling the Winepress of God's Wrath

Although the following passage is notoriously difficult to interpret, we can safely rule out a violent Jesus.

> I looked, and there before me was a white cloud, and seated on the cloud was one like a son of man with a crown of gold on his head and a sharp sickle in his hand. Then another angel came out of the

temple and called in a loud voice to him who was sitting on the cloud, "Take your sickle and reap, because the time to reap has come, for the harvest of the earth is ripe." So he who was seated on the cloud swung his sickle over the earth, and the earth was harvested.

Another angel came out of the temple in heaven, and he too had a sharp sickle. Still another angel, who had charge of the fire, came from the altar and called in a loud voice to him who had the sharp sickle, "Take your sharp sickle and gather the clusters of grapes from the earth's vine, because its grapes are ripe." The angel swung his sickle on the earth, gathered its grapes and threw them into the great winepress of God's wrath. They were trampled in the winepress outside the city, and blood flowed out of the press, rising as high as the horses' bridles for a distance of 1,600 stadia. (Rev. 14:14-20)

Note the clear distinction between what Jesus ("the one like a son of man") does in the first paragraph and what the angel does in the second. Jesus harvests the earth, but he is not involved in the winepress of God's wrath. He throws nothing into it. The angel does that.

To reap a harvest, particularly one that is ripe, is a positive thing. It means to gather the good crop. As N.T. Wright contends, "there should be no doubt that this passage, describing the harvest and the vintage, is meant to be an occasion of great, uninhibited joy. We would need a huge amount of evidence to force us to say anything else."[21] So the symbolism in the first paragraph has nothing to do with condemnation or punishment. It's about Jesus gathering the faithful to abide with him in God's kingdom for eternity. The harvest is ripe because the time has come for God's followers to be saved.

The context surrounding this passage supports this conclusion. The preceding verses announce the fall of Babylon and the defeat of the beast's followers before declaring that God's followers will, from now on, find rest from their labor (vv. 8-13). Then we have our passage, wherein Jesus ushers God's followers into eternal life and the angel kicks Satan's followers out of God's city ("They were trampled in the winepress outside the city"). Immediately thereafter, we find the faithful in heaven singing songs of praise and victory (15:1-4).

Many other New Testament passages also positively reference a metaphorical harvest, sometimes even in a similar context. After witnessing crowds that were harassed and helpless, Jesus had compassion on them and told his disciples, "The harvest is plentiful but the workers are few. Ask the Lord of the harvest, therefore, to send out workers into his harvest field" (Matt. 9:36-38). In a parable, Jesus compared God's kingdom to a man who scatters seed on the ground, watches the soil produce grain by itself, and "as soon as the grain is ripe, he puts the sickle to it, because the harvest has come" (Mark 4:26-29). On another occasion, Jesus said to his disciples, "Open your eyes and look at the fields! They are ripe for harvest. Even now the one who reaps draws a wage and harvests a crop for eternal life" (John 4:35-36). Similarly, Paul urged the Galatians to "not become weary in doing good, for at the proper time we will reap a harvest if we do not give up" (Gal. 6:9). He also told the church in Rome he had planned to visit them "in order that I might have a harvest among you" (Rom. 1:13). And on numerous other occasions, New Testament writers referred to a "harvest of righteousness" (James 3:18; Heb. 12:11; 2 Cor. 9:10).

This is one reasonable way to interpret this challenging passage. Jesus performs the nonviolent job of gathering the faithful to abide with him in God's kingdom forever. The angel, meanwhile, performs the metaphorically violent job of banishing from God's kingdom all of those who persist in unloving behavior. In Eller's words, "It is a double harvest: a positive grain harvest of blessing and a negative grape (wine) harvest of 'wrath.'"[22]

Here's a slightly different interpretation to consider: Maybe those trampled in the winepress of God's wrath aren't his enemies but his followers. The passage doesn't specify who does the trampling or whose blood flows from the press. If it is the blood of God's enemies, this is the only place in Revelation where the word *blood* is used to denote the blood of God's enemies, instead of his followers. The trampling occurs "outside the city," which may allude to where others crucified and shed Jesus's blood: "Jesus also suffered outside the city gate to make the people holy through his own blood" (Heb. 13:12). Everywhere else in Revelation, God's judgment is symbolically represented not in the act of crushing grapes but in making the wicked drink the wine of crushed grapes.[23] In other words, he directs his wrath not toward the crushed grapes but toward those who trample them. So maybe the trampled grapes are Christian martyrs (who are being harvested) and those who trample them are their killers. Christian self-sacrifice is, after all, one of Revelation's most prominent themes.

Don't be misled by Revelation's references to God's "wrath." It's one of his better characteristics. It means he hates evil and injustice. It means he loves his creation and wants to see it thrive and therefore despises everything that thwarts its flourishing, like violence, bloodshed, oppression, exploitation, deceit, envy, greed, idolatry, and death. If God didn't want everyone and everything to have life and have it abundantly, he wouldn't get angry at such unloving behaviors. Praise God for his wrath! It is an essential part of his goodness. And it only needs to be feared if you want to persist in acting unlovingly.

This is also true for God's judgment and punishment. They are good things. They mean God fights injustice. He judges it, punishes it, and sets it right. Praise God for his judgment and punishment! They arise from his love, not from some arbitrary, selfish, jealous, or vengeful bloodlust. What kind of God would he be if he didn't combat things like racism, theft, child abuse, slavery, rape, murder, and war?

But please don't jump to conclusions about how God's wrath, judgment, punishment, and correction operate on a metaphysical level. None of them necessarily require God's use of violence. As theologians like Greg Boyd have demonstrated, it is reasonable, rational, biblical, and theologically sound to conclude that God achieves such things not by directly imposing them himself but by turning evildoers over to the natural consequences of their injustice, by allowing such behaviors to run their natural course, by permitting the disobedient way of life to self-destruct.[24] So maybe God enforces justice not through direct intervention but by channeling human injustice, by ensuring that it, like all things, is put to work for good.[25] Maybe God designed the universe to work in such a way that sin is its own punishment. The Bible, including Revelation, contains an intriguing amount of supporting evidence for such a theory.

So yes, God and Jesus both get angry at injustice. They both judge it to be wrong. But neither their wrath nor their judgment symbolizes violence. Instead, they symbolize a hatred of violence. Furthermore, all throughout the Bible, only God—not Jesus or his

followers—punishes injustice.[26] And even then, God doesn't
necessarily act violently when doing so. Sure, he may "use" violence
indirectly by channeling it, but as Paul pointed out, God uses "all
things" in such a way (Rom. 8:28). To use something someone else
does is not to do it yourself.

Whatever meaning you derive from this passage or however you
interpret God's wrath in general, one thing is clear in this passage
about trampling the winepress of God's wrath: Jesus doesn't use
violence. Even if this weren't clear, we should never interpret a single
ambiguous passage in a way that contradicts numerous other, clearer
passages.

And with that, we've covered every scene in Revelation wherein
Jesus is possibly violent. All other violence that may be attributed to
God's team comes either from God himself or an angel. Jesus only
ever wields and fights with a sword *from his mouth* and only ever battles
and defeats the beast and earthly kings. Satan and Babylon are
disposed of by other means.

What Revelation Demands of Christians

Even if we interpret the actions of Jesus, God, and the angels
literally and violently, nothing in Revelation instructs Christians to
use violence or depicts them doing so. The opposite is true.

As discussed earlier, Revelation calls Christians to faithfulness,
demanding that we remain obedient amidst the world's competing
ideologies—particularly the ideology of empire—and do so even to
the point of martyrdom, if necessary. This is how Christians
"conquer" and become "victorious." "Be faithful, even to the point
of death," commands God, "and I will give you life as your victor's
crown" (2:10). To remain faithful is to conquer, and to conquer is to
remain faithful.[27]

But this raises a question: Faithfulness to whom or to what?
Well, to state the obvious, faithfulness to God and his will. That is to
say, faithfulness to the way of Jesus, who perfectly revealed God and
his will.

Revelation connects faithfulness to Jesus both implicitly and
explicitly. Within the first five verses, John declares him to be "the
faithful witness" (1:5), a fact he reiterates two more times (3:14;
19:11). Throughout the book, God's followers are referred to as

those who "follow the Lamb wherever he goes" (14:4), who "remain faithful to Jesus" (14:12), and who bear testimony to and about Jesus (12:17; 17:6; 19:10; 20:4). Jesus promises to reward those who do *his* will (2:26). God's faithful follow Jesus, not God himself or the angels, into battle against the kings of the earth (17:14; 19:13-14). They triumph as Jesus triumphed (3:21), "by the blood of the Lamb and by the word of their testimony" (12:11). They earn a place in heaven by suffering like Jesus did (7:14-15; 20:4) and by having their "names written in the Lamb's book of life" (21:27).

In short, faithfulness is how God's followers fight and Jesus defines clearly what it means to be faithful. Therefore, we wage war on evil by remaining faithful to Jesus's commands and example. Again, Revelation is not about providing Christians with a decipherable guide map of end-time events, but rather about promoting discipleship in the lives of its readers—then and now.

Furthermore, to be faithful to the way of Jesus means to be faithful to what he taught and exemplified *in the Gospels*. It does not mean faithfulness to some new Jesus or some new ethics revealed in Revelation.

Revelation doesn't teach new ethics. It encourages obedience to what Jesus has already taught, which it assumes its readers already know. This is why it contains tons of conclusory admonitions to simply be faithful and obey but almost no explanatory ethical instructions.[28] Revelation doesn't command us to care for the poor, turn the other cheek, or love our enemies because it's written to people who already know that's what God wants them to do, and who only need to be encouraged to keep at it or prodded to get with it.

Revelation doesn't issue new marching orders. It commands us to follow existing orders. And to identify those orders, we need to look to Jesus's life and teachings as recorded in the rest of the New Testament, particularly the Gospels. This makes sense. To deduce how Jesus conquered and wants us to conquer, we need to analyze the historical account of his conquering.

Revelation is nonsensical unless Jesus's gospel actions are the standard of faithfulness. Had Jesus not already demonstrated faithfulness (during his time on earth) and had John not intended for those past actions to define faithfulness, then Revelation's admonitions to follow Jesus, coupled with its lack of explanation as to precisely what that means for our behavior, would be irrational. Revelation's repeated references to Jesus's faithfulness and victory in the past tense would also not make sense. The flawed logic would be akin to an Old Testament writer who commanded God's followers to be faithful to Jesus prior to Jesus's birth—before anyone knew what that meant or what ethics it required.

Plus, not every biblical writer can say everything. Many, including John in Revelation, build upon what has already been said and done. In this sense, John never intended for Revelation to be a treatise on ethics. Nonetheless, to the small extent that it contains explicit ethical instructions, they are located in the messages to the seven churches—not in John's visions—and they echo Jesus's gospel teachings, commanding things like love, faith, service, patience, and repentance.[29]

At this point, what Christlike faithfulness means for our use of violence should be clear. It manifests itself in an entirely nonviolent way of life.[30]

As Revelation itself points out, Jesus triumphed by being slain, not by slaying. He conquered as a lamb, not a lion. He could unlock the scroll because he had been slaughtered, not because he had slaughtered. Instead of somehow employing violence more justly than his enemy, he refrained from violence altogether. Rather than forcefully resisting violence, he self-sacrificially absorbed it. He took up his cross, not a sword—or even a shield. He fought and won by dying for God's enemies, not by killing them. Instead of protecting his life at the expense of those who threatened him, he laid it down for them. He chose to have his own innocent blood shed—even to the point of death—rather than shed the blood of the guilty. He was willing to die for truth and justice and the advancement of God's kingdom on earth, but not to kill for those things. Jesus's response to violence was not more violence. It was self-sacrificial love.

Revelation calls God's followers to the same nonviolent faithfulness. It praises and promises rewards for the slain, not the slayers.[31] It encourages God's followers to absorb and endure violent persecution, not to retaliate in kind.[32] It instructs them to not fear death because Jesus has already conquered it and holds power over it.[33] Its models of faithfulness are those who suffered and died bearing living witness to the truth of Jesus's way of life, not those who died trying to violently combat evil.[34] It memorializes prophets and martyrs, not fallen soldiers.[35]

Revelation never depicts God's followers carrying weapons of any type, not even swords protruding from their mouths.[36] Instead, it portrays them wearing robes made white by Jesus's own blood, which is a symbol of faithful suffering and martyrdom.[37]

Look at the role of Christians in each of Revelation's figurative battles against God's enemies. They are never even symbolically depicted fighting the beast, earthly kings, the false prophet, Babylon, or the dragon. Instead, it is always God, Jesus, or an angel who does the metaphorical fighting and killing.[38] Christians are only ever portrayed as being persecuted by God's enemies and encouraged to endure it.[39] On the single occasion in which they are summarily declared to have defeated an enemy (the dragon), they are said to have "triumphed over him by the blood of the Lamb and by the word of their testimony; they did not love their lives so much as to shrink from death" (12:11). And the two times they are pictured with Jesus when he defeats his enemies, they are never depicted doing any actual fighting.[40] They simply follow Jesus "wherever he goes" (14:4).

Returning to Jesus's faithfulness, it also manifested itself in a complete avoidance of governmental power. He never even collaborated with it indirectly. He rejected Satan's offer (which the Bible more accurately terms a *temptation*) of control over all the kingdoms of the world.[41] When a crowd tried to thrust political power upon him by forcing him to be king, he fled to the mountains.[42] When the disciples asked Jesus who among them would be given the most power and prestige in his kingdom, he instructed them not to "lord" over others like the "rulers of the Gentiles" (Matt. 20:25). Maybe most importantly, when a Roman governor accused Jesus of leading an insurrection, Jesus declared that his kingdom and his followers do not employ such earthly power—they do not fight with violence.[43]

As we will explore in more detail in Chapter 8, the eschewal of governmental power was a prominent theme throughout Jesus's ministry. At numerous points during his life, he could have directly employed governmental power, or indirectly partnered with it, to ostensibly further God's will, but he didn't. He advanced God's kingdom on earth by embodying, living, and speaking the kingdom, not by forcing it on others. He fought injustice through example, not control. He overcame evil by refusing to partake in its means, not by wielding its weapons more effectively or more justly. He refused to use political power to maintain social order, promote the common good, or ensure that history would turn out right. Instead, he humbly and patiently entrusted such things—the things we think we need to use government power for—to God, thereby bearing witness to his father's control over them. Despite all the material good he could seemingly have accomplished with governmental power, he shunned it.

Revelation calls God's followers to the same abstention. It never depicts Christians controlling or partnering with nations to advance God's kingdom and never instructs them to ensure—in any way, shape, or form—that government does its God-ordained job, upholds social morality, enforces social justice, or defends religious freedom. On the contrary, it portrays all earthly kings and kingdoms as God's enemies.

A voice from heaven declared, "Come out of [Babylon], my people, so that you will not share in her sins, so that you will not receive any of her plagues; for her sins are piled up to heaven, and God has remembered her crimes" (18:4-5). To "come out," as it is intended here, does not mean to physically leave earthly nations. It means to disassociate from their domineering, violence-driven way of life. Revelation instructs Christians not to revolt against government but to refuse to partake in its coercive rule. It also promises that those who receive the mark of the beast (which represents imperial power) will experience God's fury, while those who refuse it will be given authority over the nations and will reign with Jesus in eternity.[44]

When the Christian martyrs cried out to God for justice, "they were told to wait a little longer" (6:10-11). Like Jesus, they had dutifully entrusted judgment and vengeance to God, but unlike Jesus, they were becoming impatient. So God instructed them to keep trusting in his control and continue refraining from taking matters into their own hands. This is one of Revelation's main objectives: to convince Christians to remain faithful to the way of Jesus and leave vengeance to God, because *he* will execute it when the time is right (after all have ample opportunity to repent).

Revelation isn't unique in this regard. Throughout Scripture, God's followers are called to leave vengeance (and any violence it may entail) to him.[45] The admonition is found in every passage people cite to justify human violence, from the Old Testament to Romans 13 and all the way through Revelation. The Bible is crystal clear on this point: judgment and vengeance belong to God alone. Our task is simply to announce them (when appropriate, and in an appropriate manner), not to execute them. To do the latter is to usurp God's authority. Eventually, he will give us authority over the nations, but not yet.[46]

Resisting the allure of government's violence-based power and control has been a struggle for God's people since the beginning. "In the Bible there is really only one story: that of a people struggling to leave empire behind and set out to follow God," write Wes Howard-Brook and Anthony Gwyther. "That story was to be relived whether in Egypt, Babylon, Rome, or elsewhere."[47] Indeed, God's followers seem stuck in a perpetual tug of war between turning to earthly kingdoms for their safety, comfort, and control and entrusting such things to him.

But if Revelation makes anything clear, it is that we advance God's kingdom on earth not by political means but by remaining faithful to the non-coercive way of Jesus. It doesn't call us to use earthly power to manage society, steer history, or ensure our own survival. It calls us to bear witness to God's control of such things, which requires living as if we really believe in his control. We show we believe by not trying to control those things ourselves. Christians wage war by embodying Jesus's way of life, not by forcing it on others. We fight and conquer not by lording over others as empires do, but by selflessly serving others. We overcome violence by refusing to perpetuate it, by depriving its fire of oxygen, not by harnessing it for "good."

We can't have it both ways. We can't wield governmental power and advance God's kingdom on earth. The two are incompatible.

Governmental power is coercion-based. It relies on violence or the threat of it, which is why governments employ policemen and soldiers to impose fines, imprisonment, or death on those who disobey their edicts. Christ's power, on the other hand, is entirely nonviolent, relying on peaceful persuasion and exemplification instead, which is why the church employs preachers and servants instead of armed personnel.

As libertarian political philosophy has long pointed out, to employ government is to employ violence. If there's no need for the use or threat of physical force, then there's no need for government. Government is, by its very nature, physical force. Don't be fooled by the often veiled and indirect character of its force or the intentions of those wielding it. Whether wielded for personal gain or to help others, its violent nature remains. The "selfless" use of physical coercion is still the use of physical coercion.

This is why Revelation compares and contrasts God's kingdom with empire. They are precise opposites in both their means and their ends. One operates through violence, the other through nonviolence. One seeks its own safety and comfort at the expense of others, the other the safety and comfort of others at its own expense. One tries to conquer the world by dominating it, the other by loving it.

Hence the reason we must choose between using governmental power and advancing God's kingdom. To be entangled in the world's power struggles is to be engaged in trying to control Satan's kingdom, and as long as we are trying to manage Satan's kingdom, we are not advancing God's.

We cannot serve two masters. Only one can receive our full faith, trust, and allegiance. The Romans knew this, which is why faith in Caesar was considered a civic virtue and why a lack of such faith was considered atheism—a crime for which the earthly Christians were often indicted.

To put your trust and faith in government and its means of ruling is to cheat on God, which is why Revelation repeatedly refers to Babylon (a great city of wealth and power built upon violence) as a prostitute with whom the kings of the earth, and others, committed adultery.[48] She sold herself to another god—the god of imperial power—in exchange for a morsel of momentary pleasure, a smidgen of temporary control, and fleeting sense of safety. We make the same mistake when we climb into bed with governmental power.

This is also why Revelation describes the 144,000 as "those who did not defile themselves with women, for they remained virgins" (14:4). John isn't talking about literal sex. He is symbolically and metaphorically referring to remaining faithfully obedient to God instead of empire, which is why the very next sentence says, "They follow the Lamb wherever he goes."

Throughout the Bible, including in Revelation, prostitution and sexual infidelity are metaphors for idolatry.[49] Similarly, throughout the New Testament, the church is occasionally referred to as the bride of Christ, meaning it is betrothed to him and him alone.[50] Its duty is to remain faithful. And as we've just seen, that includes declining governmental power, for to employ such power is to ally with Satan's means of ruling.

For these reasons and others, the whole point of God's war against Satan is to eradicate earthly kingdoms and their modus operandi. He wants to replace Satan's way of ruling the world, as embodied in violence-driven governmental power, with his way of ruling the world, as embodied in the always-loving and wholly non-coercive slaughtered lamb. He sent Jesus to earth to become its sole king and to rule it with nonviolent love for all eternity, thereby banishing earthly governments to the dustbin of history. This is why Revelation repeatedly declares Jesus to be the world's rightful ruler, pits him against earthly kings, and ultimately depicts him triumphing over them.[51]

Notice that Jesus didn't redeem governmental power. He didn't restore it to its proper role, ensure that it was placed in the right hands, or otherwise harness it for good. He defeated it. "And having disarmed the powers and authorities, he made a public spectacle of them, triumphing over them by the cross" (Col. 2:15). His was a victory over violence itself, not merely its improper use.

Most importantly, Jesus achieved victory through love and for love. He fought and conquered through his testimony, by bearing witness to the truth in both word (symbolized by a sword coming out of his mouth) and deed (symbolized by a slaughtered lamb).

To summarize what Revelation demands of Christians, nothing in Revelation instructs or even implicitly encourages the use of violence, not now or ever. Precisely the opposite is the case. From every angle, whether literal or symbolic, Revelation advocates faithfulness to Christlike nonviolence. There are a few debatable and difficult-to-understand aspects of Revelation, but this isn't one of them. The book of Revelation calls believers to the same nonviolent ethics that the rest of the New Testament requires, not to a more just or more effective type of violence.

Even if Revelation can be accurately read as depicting the use of actual violence by God, Jesus, or angels at the end of history, nothing about their future actions justifies human violence today. Everywhere and always in the New Testament, including in Revelation, we are called to obey and mimic the Jesus of the Gospels, not the God, Jesus, or angels of the violent parables or Revelation. Even if God plans to issue new instructions to use violence at some point in the future (and we have no reason to believe that he does), our current orders are to live and die like Jesus did—nonviolently.

Furthermore, even if we conclude that God, Jesus, or angels *do* use violence, their violence is always opposed to human violence. It is always employed to discourage and end human violence. Therefore, although Revelation's message about God's use or non-use of violence may not be as clear as we'd like, its message about human violence is clear: God hates human violence, and he will judge, punish, and eradicate it.

"The book often thought to overturn the ethic of nonviolence," concludes Sprinkle, "is actually its greatest defender."[52]

Reading Revelation Nonviolently

The key to reading Revelation nonviolently lies in respecting its literary genre by reading it symbolically, and then interpreting its symbols through the lens of the Gospels. Such an approach reveals its nonviolent themes. On the other hand, a genre-violating, literalistic, Gospel-disregarding interpretation completely misses the book's radical antiviolence message and instead causes the reader to walk away with a contradictory pro-violence impression.

Yes, John uses violent symbolism. But he also uses nonviolent symbolism. And he combines them in a way that subverts violence. He reveals violence to be Satan's means, not God's; powerless, not redemptive; beaten, not victorious. He exposes the myth of redemptive violence and unveils the truth of redemptive love.

Yes, Revelation's big-picture analogy describes warfare and violent conflict. Like the rest of the New Testament, it adopts the Old Testament's warfare worldview and continues its "holy war" tradition, both of which convey vital messages about God (e.g., that he despises and combats injustice). But also like the rest of the New Testament, Revelation redefines key elements of the Old Testament's perspective, particularly its view of violence. When John is told that the "Lion of the tribe of Judah" has triumphed, he hears the Old Testament's perspective on how to fight and conquer. But when he looks at the conqueror with his new Gospel glasses, he sees a slaughtered lamb and a new way of battling evil. Through such nuanced symbolism, John is telling us that the Old Testament's predictions of a conquering Messiah were correct, but its expectations for *how* he (and his followers) would conquer were not.

According to the entire New Testament, including Revelation, Jesus overcame violence and death, not by avoiding or controlling them, but by allowing them to do their worst to him—crucify him— and then rising from the dead, thereby demonstrating his power over them. He allowed himself to be "conquered" by violence and death so that he could show the world what real conquering looks like: uncompromising, self-sacrificial, nonviolent love—even unto death. Or, as John would say, it looks like lamb power, not lion power.

This is one of the mysteries unlocked by Jesus in the Gospels and symbolically highlighted in Revelation through Jesus's opening of the scroll. The most powerful force in the universe is Christlike love, not violence. But it took Jesus to reveal it. For the first time in recorded history, he associated self-sacrificial nonviolence with victory and success. Without him, the power of love would still be disguised as apparent weakness while the apparent power of violence would still be hiding its true weakness.

This is why the first sentence of John's book introduces itself as "the revelation from Jesus Christ." It is a report of what Jesus revealed—that God, not empire, is in control; that he, not Satan, has won, is winning, and will win; and that self-sacrificial love, not violence, conquers all. As Zahnd concludes, "The book of Revelation is not where the good news of the gospel goes to die" or "where the gospel becomes the anti-gospel" but "where the good news of the gospel finds its most creative expression."[53]

Not only is a nonviolent reading of Revelation possible, it is also responsible, rational, and scripturally based. It respects the book's historical and literary contexts, comports with the trajectory of the greater biblical narrative, confirms what the rest of the New Testament teaches, and, most importantly, is Christ-centered. Its conclusions arise from what came before it, the bigger picture within which it sits, and the axis around which it revolves—not from a few isolated, obscure, and ambiguous images. As a result, it is more theologically sound than any violent interpretation.

A symbolic, nonviolent reading of Revelation also produces better fruit than a literal, violent reading. After all, if Jesus will annihilate all non-Christians upon his return, what does it matter if we kill a few thousand here or there? And if God will eventually destroy the earth, why should we inconvenience ourselves with taking caring of it today?

So you have a choice. You can read Revelation violently or nonviolently. But why would you interpret it violently when there is an equally rational way to interpret it nonviolently? You don't even have to surrender your belief in God's wrath, judgment, or victory to do so.

---

[1] Rev. 1:1-2. As Eller explains in his commentary *The Most Revealing Book of the Bible: Making Sense Out of Revelation*, when John introduces his letter as "the revelation from Jesus Christ," he intends it to convey two points. He wants Jesus "to be understood as the Revealer, the prime possessor and bearer of the revelation," and also "the content of the revelation. Jesus Christ is both the Revealer and that which is being revealed." See page 12.

[2] Rev. 7:10; 12:10.

[3] Rev. 1:5; 17:14; 19:13-21.

[4] Rev. 12:11, 17; 14:4-5, 12; 17:6, 14-17; 19:10, 13-14; 20:4, 6.

[5] N. T. Wright, *Revelation for Everyone*, 1008.

[6] M. Eugene Boring, "Narrative Christology in the Apocalypse," CBQ 54, no. 4 (1992): 708.

[7] Richard B. Hays, *Revelation and the Politics of Apocalyptic Interpretation*, ed. Richard B. Hays and Stefan Alkier (Baylor University Press, 2012), 1854, Kindle.

[8] Preston Sprinkle, *Fight: A Christian Case for Non-Violence* (David C. Cook, 2013), 2746, Kindle.

[9] Rev. 17:6; 18:24.

[10] Rev. 1:16; 2:16; 19:15, 21.

[11] Ps. 57:4; Ps. 59:7; 64:3.

[12] Rev. 2:24; 3:7, 9, 14; 6:10; 12:9; 13:1-6, 14; 14:5; 15:3; 16:7; 17:3; 18:23; 19:2, 9, 11, 20; 20:3, 7, 9-10; 21:5, 27; 22:6, 15.

[13] Boyd explains: "Beyond the previously mentioned considerations regarding the symbolic nature of John's word-pictures, the symbolic nature of this macabre scene is made quite clear by the fact that though this passage

depicts all nations as being defeated (Rev 19:15, 19) and all rebels as being devoured by birds (Rev 19:18, 21), we continue to read about these nations and rebels in subsequent chapters (Rev 20:8, 22:11). Indeed, we are even given some hope that the nations and rebels who are slain and devoured in Revelation 19 will eventually be redeemed (Rev 21:24–26, 22:2). While no one who persists in wickedness can enter the heavenly city, the gates of the city will never be shut (Rev 21:25, 27)." See *The Crucifixion of the Warrior God*, 13962.

[14] Interestingly, the same is true for the "final battle" with the other human-led institution in Revelation: Babylon. When it is defeated, no actual fighting occurs. It simply self-destructs.

[15] John made this clear way back in Chapter 5 when he declared Jesus worthy to open the scroll because he "has triumphed," a fact he reminds us of in this passage by pointing out Jesus's already bloody robe.

[16] Vernard Eller, *The Most Revealing Book of the Bible: Making Sense Out of Revelation* (Grand Rapids, MI: Wm. B. Eerdmans Publishing Co., 1975), 32.

[17] Brian D. McLaren, *A New Kind of Christianity: Ten Questions That Are Transforming the Faith*, Reprint Edition (HarperCollins, 2010), 2111, Kindle.

[18] See the last chapter in my book *The Old Testament Case for Nonviolence*.

[19] Zahnd, *Sinners in the Hands of a Loving God*, 2270.

[20] Some interpreters have claimed that this first rider represents Jesus. I don't think so. First, the rider carries a bow, a weapon that is nowhere else in Scripture associated with Jesus. Second, such a conclusion doesn't fit with the fact that all the other riders represent forces of evil. Third, while the rider shares two symbolic details with Jesus (he wears a crown like Jesus and he rides out to conquer on a white horse as Jesus does later in Revelation), so does all evil. "Evil is not sheer ugliness but rather counterfeit beauty," writes Eller. "Evil comes through as a perverted, mirror image of the Good. And this is the explanation of its power and attractiveness." (See page 36 in *The Most Revealing Book of the Bible*.) Instead, I believe, in accordance with N.T. Wright, that the rider on the white horse most likely "symbolizes the conquering kings of the earth who have charged to and fro, overcoming mighty nations and claiming sovereignty (the 'crown') over them." (See Kindle location 1147 in *Revelation for Everyone*.) However, even if the first rider does represent Jesus, notice he does not commit any violence or sow any specific destruction. He merely rides "out as a conqueror bent on conquest."

[21] N. T. Wright, *Revelation for Everyone*, 2355.

[22] Eller, *The Most Revealing Book of the Bible*, 143.

[23] Rev. 14:10; 16:6; 17:6.

[24] See Boyd's *The Crucifixion of the Warrior God: Interpreting the Old Testament's Violent Portraits of God in Light of the Cross*, or his less-academic version *Cross Vision: How the Crucifixion of Jesus Makes Sense of Old Testament Violence.*

[25] Rom. 8:28.

[26] Highly astute readers will note that although Jesus isn't the one who throws the grapes into the winepress of God's wrath in this passage (14:14-20), he does "tread the winepress of the fury of the wrath of God" in the part of Chapter 19 discussed above. I think there's a small but significant distinction between the two. In Chapter 19, where Jesus treads the winepress, no one is thrown into it and no blood flows from it. In other words, in Chapter 19, God's wrath does not get imposed. It does not take the form of punishment. Therefore, to say that Jesus treads the winepress of God's wrath without depicting any associated punishment is simply to say that Jesus, like God, hates injustice, a fact we've just learned has nothing to do with using violence.

[27] This is what it means to proclaim the cross a victory, as we did in Chapter 5. The victory lies in remaining faithful unto death, in dying instead of compromising to survive.

[28] For verses that summarily advocate obedience to God, see 2:26 and 3:2-3, 8. For verses that summarily define God's people as those who obey him, see 12:17, 14:12, and 20:6. For verses that summarily warn us of judgment according to our deeds, see 2:23, 20:12-13, and 22:12.

[29] To put it another way, although Revelation isn't a treatise on the ethics of violence, it definitely has something to say about the subject. It encourages us to remain faithful to what Jesus has already taught about it and looks forward to the eradication of violence, to a world without violence, to the kingdom of God.

[30] John likely didn't even consider the possibility that using violent illustrations, in an effort to metaphorically communicate the reality of Jesus's war against and defeat of evil, could be interpreted as advocating for, or even endorsing, actual human violence. For John, Jesus's antiviolence was obvious and well-known.

[31] Rev. 6:9-11; 7:13-15; 20:4-6; 22:14.

[32] Rev. 13:10.

[33] Rev. 1:17-18; 2:10; 11:1–13.

[34] Rev. 1:9; 2:13; 7:13-15; 12:11; 17:6.

[35] Of course, martyrdom isn't the goal. God doesn't want us to seek our own death for the sake of dying. The goal is faithful obedience, regardless of the cost. God calls us not to die but to be willing to die if necessary to avoid complicity with evil. Death is simply a *possible* byproduct of uncompromising faithfulness.

[36] By "God's followers," I mean Christians generally. There is one instance (11:3-7) in which two unique, God-appointed witnesses are said to possess the ability to defend themselves with fire *from their mouths* and the power to unleash plagues. But they are never depicted doing so, and instead are martyred. N.T. Wright believes these two prophets are reminiscent of Moses and Elijah, each of whom stood up to oppression and idolatry by speaking the truth and calling forth plagues. "What John is saying," he contends, "is that the prophetic witness of the church, in the great tradition of Moses and Elijah, will perform powerful signs and thereby torment the surrounding unbelievers, but that the climax of their work will be their martyr-death ...." See Kindle location 1777 in *Revelation for Everyone*.

[37] Rev. 6:9-11; 7:14; 19:8, 14; 22:14.

[38] Rev. 16:1-21; 17:16-17; 18:8, 20-21; 19:1-2, 11-21; 20:1-3, 7-10, 13-14.

[39] Rev. 13:9-10; 14:12-13; 17:6; 18:24; 19:1-2.

[40] Rev. 17:12-14; 19:14.

[41] Luke 4:5-8.

[42] John 6:1-15.

[43] Luke 18:33-36.

[44] Rev. 14:9-12; 16:2; 20:4.

[45] Deut. 32:35; 1 Sam. 24:12-13; Isa. 30:18; 35:4; Prov. 20:22; Luke 6:37; 1 Pet. 2:19-23; Rom. 2:1-3; 12:19; 13:4; Heb. 10:30; 1 Cor. 5:12-13.

[46] Rev. 2:26-27; 20:4.

[47] Wes Howard-Brook and Anthony Gwyther, *Unveiling Empire: Reading Revelation Then and Now* (Orbis Books, 1999), 4727, Kindle.

[48] Rev. 14:8; 17:2, 5-6; 18:3-4, 7, 9-20, 24; 19:1-8.

[49] Exod. 34:15-16; Lev. 17:7; Num. 15:39; Deut. 31:16; Judg. 8:27; 1 Chron. 5:25; 2 Chron. 21:11; Isa. 1:21; 23:17; Jer. 2:20; 13:27; Ezek. 16:23-30; 23:7; Hosea 4:12; 5:4; Rev. 2:20-23; 14:8; 17:2, 4-5; 18:3, 9; 19:2.

[50] Matt. 25:1-13; Mark 2:19-20; Luke 5:34-35; John 3:28-30; Rev. 18:23; 19:7; 21:2, 9; 22:17.

[51] Rev. 1:4-5; 2:26-27; 3:14; 11:15; 12:5; 17:12-14; 19:15-16, 19-21.

[52] Sprinkle, *Fight*, 2709.

[53] Zahnd, *Sinners in the Hands of a Loving God*, 2373.

CHAPTER 8

A NEW KIND OF KING

In Chapter 5, we explored how the Bible frames life in terms of a great war between God's and Satan's kingdoms, and how God sent Jesus to reestablish his rule by becoming king on earth, which he did via his life, death, and resurrection. In this chapter, we will inspect the character of Jesus's kingship and reign, primarily from the perspective of violence.

To set the scene, recall that Jesus was born into an atmosphere of great political expectation. God had promised the Israelites a messianic king who would rule the entire world forever and king-related questions permeated everyone's thoughts: When will the new king arrive? How will he establish his kingdom? What type of ruler will he be? And so on. How Jesus answered these types of questions reveals much about his relationship with violence and its role in God's kingdom.

Minority Options

As a member of a minority sect, Jesus had four main options for advancing God's kingdom under Roman occupation. Like the Zealots, he could have become a violent revolutionary and waged holy warfare against Rome. In the manner of the Essenes, he could have denounced secular life and withdrawn from mainstream society to live in monastic seclusion until God defeated his enemies. As did the Pharisees, he could have acquiesced to Rome's politics but disconnected from its daily customs by adopting a lifestyle of religious legalism focused on cultivating personal purity. Or he could have adopted the "realistic" and "practical" strategy of the Sadducees, who tried to make the best of a bad situation by collaborating with the existing powers whenever it was pragmatically prudent.

Jesus did none of these things. He didn't adopt the strategy of withdrawal, of waiting for God to act without human involvement. He advocated personal holiness, but he viewed religious legalism as a barrier to rather than a means of achieving holiness. And he definitely didn't integrate himself into the established power structures so that he could change them from within, despite the popularity of that option among Christians today.

On the other hand, Jesus had much in common with the Zealots, particularly their revolutionary spirit. Like them, he denounced the present system, subversively stoked rebellion, sought followers who were fanatically committed to his ideals, and was not afraid to die for his cause. In fact, many of his contemporaries viewed him as a Zealot, and the Romans executed him as one.

But Jesus was no Zealot. He differed in one crucial respect: he was nonviolent. Unlike the Zealots, he didn't believe the sword was the solution or that God's will needed to be—or even could be—implemented through superior force. He shared the Zealots' distaste for the Roman Empire and their zeal for reestablishing God's kingdom, but not their means of opposition. "You heard that it was said, 'An eye for an eye, and a tooth for a tooth.' But I say to you: don't use violence to resist evil!" (Matt. 5:38-39).[1]

Given their similarities and shared goal, Jesus's rejection of the Zealot option highlights nonviolence as a vital component of his kingship. He didn't reject the way of the Zealot because he wanted to avoid conflict, was afraid of persecution, thought he might lose the battle, or believed his sole purpose was to die on the cross for sin. He rejected it because fighting, conquering, and ruling through violence is how evil operates, not how God operates. He rejected it not because it would have failed, but because its success would not have accomplished much. Instead of establishing God's kingdom, it would have merely traded one version of Satan's kingdom for another. Sure, life in the new kingdom would be a little safer and a bit more comfortable, but the cycle of violence would remain intact. Jesus's reign would depend on his continued use of superior violence, and at his death, his kingdom would immediately become susceptible to defeat.

Jesus rejected the Zealot option not because it was too radical but because it wasn't radical enough.

Political Power

Jesus also had another power option, one that most minority members never have: political power. Early in Jesus's ministry, Satan tempted him with control of all the kingdoms of the world:

> The devil led him up to a high place and showed him in an instant all the kingdoms of the world. And he said to him, "I will give you all their authority and splendor; it has been given to me, and I can give it to anyone I want to. If you worship me, it will all be yours."
>
> Jesus answered, "It is written: 'Worship the Lord your God and serve him only.'" (Luke 4:5-8)

Think of all the good Jesus could have accomplished with such vast political power. Imagine the pragmatic difference he could have made. As Boyd notes, "He could have immediately put in place all the wisest and most just laws. The painful oppression of his own people could have instantly been brought to an end. He could have ended world hunger. He could have commanded an end to bloodshed around the world."[2] And he could have done it all without having to live the hard life of an itinerant preacher or having to be tortured to death on a cross. Who among us would not have taken that deal?

Yet Jesus rejected it! He didn't say, "Hey, great idea! Why didn't I think of that? Now I can be much more effective." Instead, he responded with a clear, definitive, forceful "NO!"

This incident proves that Jesus's refusal to seek or wield political power was no oversight. After arriving on earth, he didn't forget about political power as a potential means of advancing God's kingdom. He consciously rejected it as ineffective, incompatible, and unworthy.

It's nearly impossible to overemphasize the significance of this event for Christians who are citizens of powerful earthly nations. Jesus was given the opportunity to employ political power in a socially responsible way—to promote the common good by instituting perfect social justice—but he declined. Despite vehemently disagreeing with how the Roman politicians were doing their God-ordained job, he never attempted to seize their power and wield it more Christianly.

Again, Jesus didn't come to make the fallen world a better version of itself, to make Satan's kingdom a bit more Christian. He came to make it something wholly different, something new. He came to remake it into the kingdom of God.

Notice how this passage implies that political power is satanic. First, it labels Satan's offer of political power a *temptation*, meaning it appealed to a desire to do something wrong. In this case, it appealed to the fallen human urge to forcefully control others via government. Second, it was a temptation *from Satan*. He, not God, wanted Jesus to wield political power. Third, Jesus didn't dispute Satan's claim to control the "authority and splendor" of all the kingdoms of the world. On the contrary, Jesus later confirmed it, albeit implicitly, when he called Satan "the prince of this world," as did Paul when he described Satan as "the god of this age" and John when he proclaimed "that the whole world is under the control of the evil one."[3] Thus, instead of snatching political power from Satan when he had the chance, Jesus rejected it for what it was—the devil's playground.

In a similar but less dramatic event involving a different type of tempter—human ones—Jesus gave the same response. After he miraculously fed five thousand people with "five small barley loves and two small fish," the grateful crowd decided to "make him king by force," so he "withdrew again to a mountain by himself" (John 6:1-15). In other words, when Jesus's own supporters attempted to crown him a traditional earthly king, when they tried to thrust political power upon him, he fled.

Furthermore, as mentioned in Chapter 2, when the disciples asked Jesus who among them would have the most political power and prestige in his kingdom, he chastised the very notion:

> You know that the rulers of the Gentiles lord it over them, and their high officials exercise authority over them. Not so with you. Instead, whoever wants to become great among you must be your servant, and whoever wants to be first must be your slave—just as the Son of Man did not come to be served, but to serve, and to give his life as a ransom for many. (Matt. 20:25-28; see also Mark 10:35-45 and Luke 22:24-30)

In a world that prioritizes ruling, Jesus says to prioritize serving. Resist the desire to control others and devote yourselves to assisting them. Stop competing to issue edicts and start washing feet. Put down your quest for a scepter and pick up a cross. Avoid the pursuit of earthly authority and embrace a life of humble service. Instead of trying to influence others by forcing your will on them, influence them through self-sacrifice. Change things from the bottom up, not the top down. Exercise power under, not power over.

Here is Jesus's political philosophy in a nutshell: Don't control; serve. His answer to how our broken world operates is not avoidance, collaboration, religion, or better violence. It is servanthood. This servanthood, rather than attempting to politically steer the course of history, is the Christian calling. "Indeed," notes Boyd, "the only reason Jesus bothered to draw attention to the way pagans 'lord over one another' was to make the point that his disciples are to do the opposite."[4]

Jesus's example and instructions in this regard couldn't have been any clearer. He came to earth as a lowly servant, not as a king, military general, rich aristocrat, or high priest. "He made himself nothing by taking the very nature of a servant, being made in human likeness" (Phil. 2:7). He rejected social prestige and power for a life of humble, undignified, self-degrading servanthood, one that involved being born in a manger, living a life of poverty, washing others' feet, caring for lepers, associating with social outcasts, and dying a humiliating, tortuous death on a cross. Jesus himself declared that he "did not come to be served, but to serve, and to give his life as a ransom for many" (Matt. 20:28).

Instead of advancing God's kingdom by ascending to political power, Jesus advanced it by descending to servanthood.

Likewise, Jesus told his followers "whoever wants to become great among you must be your servant, and whoever wants to be first must be your slave" (Matt. 20:26-27). "Anyone who wants to be first must be the very last, and the servant of all" (Mark 9:35). "The greatest among you will be your servant. For those who exalt themselves will be humbled, and those who humble themselves will be exalted" (Matt. 23:11-12).[5] On one occasion, after he had finished washing the disciples' feet, he told them, "I have set you an example that you should do as I have done for you. Very truly I tell you, no servant is greater than his master, nor is a messenger greater than the one who sent him" (John 13:15-16).

Jesus's apostles seemed to get the point. They spread this anti-lording and pro-servanthood sentiment throughout the New Testament.[6] But that's not to say that the sentiment is unique to the

New Testament. Even the Old Testament sends a consistent anti-ruling message, from God creating a perfect world in which he gave humans dominion over nature but not each other (Gen. 1) to his explicit warning about the exploitative nature of earthly rulers when Israel first requested a king (1 Sam. 8) to the eventual and total failure of Israel's kingship experiment.

Jesus had such an aversion to political power that he wouldn't even participate in political debates. Whenever others asked him a politically charged question, he did not answer directly but instead redirected the discussion back to the kingdom of God.

The famous "Render unto Caesar" incident provides a good example. Intending to trap Jesus into either getting arrested by the Romans or alienating the occupied Jews, the Pharisees asked him, "Is it right to pay the imperial tax to Caesar or not?" (Matt. 22:17). Jesus, aware of their scheme, asked to see the coin used to pay the tax, held it up, and then asked them whose image and inscription was on it (vv. 19-20). "Caesar's," they answered. "So give back to Caesar what is Caesar's, and to God what is God's," replied Jesus (v. 21). Boyd explains the significance of this exchange:

> Do you see how Jesus ingeniously replaced the leaders' political question with his own Kingdom question? Holding up the idolatrous coin, Jesus was in essence saying: "Are we Jews really going to bicker with each other about how much of this idolatrous metal we should cling to? Since it all bears Caesar's image, give all back to him! The only important question we ought to be wrestling with is whether or not we are giving back to God all that bears his image—namely, our whole self."[7]

Jesus's indifference to his contemporaries' political power struggles was stunning. Many Christians today would label him coldhearted and irresponsible, if not guilty of aiding and abetting evil. Not once did he instruct his followers to politically impose Christian values. He never even explicitly condemned the Roman policies regarding wealth inequality, abortion, or slavery, let alone lobbied to change them. (Of course, everything Jesus said and did implicitly opposed such injustices, but he wanted his followers to combat them through their loving example, not through violence-based political coercion.)

The apostle Paul took Jesus's renunciation of political power so seriously he encouraged fellow believers to refrain from even suing one another. "If any of you has a dispute with another, do you dare to take it before the ungodly for judgment instead of before the Lord's people?" (1 Cor. 6:1). If you have disputes, why "do you ask for a ruling from those whose way of life is scorned in the church?" (v. 4). "The very fact that you have lawsuits among you means you have been completely defeated already. Why not rather be wronged? Why not rather be cheated?" (v. 7). Tough questions.

Jesus also didn't want to be known as the Messiah until he could redefine the term to exclude violence. When he began his ministry, his first-century audience understood and expected messiahship to be associated with warfare, conquest, and political power. Consequently, had Jesus announced his messiahship prior to establishing his pacifism, he likely would have been arrested as a Zealot leader by the Romans, who would have thought they were neutralizing him before he could gather his troops and begin his violent insurrection.

This is one reason why Jesus waited until the end of his ministry to acknowledge that he was the promised Messiah and why he ordered those who realized it earlier, including his disciples, not to tell anyone.[8] He wasn't trying to stifle anyone's evangelistic zeal. He was trying to avoid premature arrest and prevent everyone from getting the wrong impression about what it meant for him to be the Messiah. He needed time to demonstrate that he wasn't mounting a violent rebellion and he didn't want to seize political power. He needed to first complete his redefinition of messianic kingship and fully disassociate it from the violence of political power.

The disciples themselves had difficulty grasping this redefinition. When Jesus first informed them that he was the Messiah, he also explained that as Messiah he would have to suffer, die, and be resurrected.[9] He knew true messiahship required such a course. But Peter didn't see it. He rebuked Jesus, saying, "Never Lord! This shall never happen to you!" (Matt. 16:22). That's not what messianic kings do. They don't suffer and die at the hands of their enemies—let alone do so prematurely, just as they are gaining momentum. They fight. They conquer. They rule.

Peter's worldview was still rooted in the myth of redemptive violence. He had not yet put on the mind of Christ. He still believed that superior violence is what will save the world, that it is the key to advancing God's kingdom on earth.

Jesus's response to Peter couldn't be more revealing. He said to him, "Get behind me, Satan! You are a stumbling block to me; you do not have in mind the concerns of God, but merely human concerns" (v. 23). Then, as if to remove all doubt, he turned to his disciples and said, "Whoever wants to be my disciple must deny themselves and take up their cross and follow me. For whoever wants to save their life will lose it, but whoever loses their life for me will find it" (vv. 24-25).

Peter tells Jesus he can't be the Messiah unless he becomes a typical earthly king. Jesus tells Peter he can't be the Messiah if he does.

Jesus's gradual acknowledgement of his messiahship was peppered with symbolic acts designed to de-violence the term. For example, when Jesus first publicly announced his divine authority, he read aloud the following well-known passage from the prophet Isaiah:

> The Spirit of the Lord is on me, because he has anointed me to proclaim good news to the poor. He has sent me to proclaim freedom for the prisoners and recovery of sight for the blind, to set the oppressed free, to proclaim the year of the Lord's favor. (Luke 4:18-19)

Such a statement was itself indicative of Jesus's unique messiahship, but what he did next was the real shocker. He promptly sat down and said, "Today this scripture is fulfilled in your hearing" (v. 21).

To understand why this was such a surprise and how it relates to Jesus's nonviolence, you have to know what Jesus *didn't* say. He stopped reading in the middle of Isaiah's sentence, right before the part that would have implicitly associated his messiahship with violence. Here's the full phrase as it appears in Isaiah 61, with the words Jesus chose not to read italicized: "to proclaim the year of the Lord's favor *and the day of vengeance of our God.*" Jesus was so concerned with disassociating his ministry from violence that he stopped mid-sentence solely to avoid any possible connection to the violence implicit in the word *vengeance*.

Jesus pulled a similar stunt when he first entered Jerusalem as king of Israel. He did so riding on a donkey, not a war horse, and surrounded by commoners waving palm branches, not accompanied by an army or a contingent of bodyguards.[10] He made his triumphant political entrance on an ass flanked by peasants, not on a powerful stallion amidst a military processional. In doing so, he fulfilled the Prophet Zechariah's claim that the Messiah would come "lowly and riding on a donkey" and would "take away the chariots from Ephraim and the warhorses from Jerusalem, and the battle bow will be broken" and would "proclaim peace to the nations" (Zech. 9:9-10).

Jesus's transportation choice and the makeup of his political parade was saturated with nonviolent symbolism. He was purposefully patterning himself after the humble, swordless Messiah that Zechariah had foretold. It was a brilliant move. Even with the benefit of hindsight, it's difficult to devise a better way to proclaim oneself the Messiah while symbolically contrasting the uniquely nonviolent nature of your kingship with that of the world.

Similarly, consider the surprisingly nonviolent evidence Jesus cited to prove he was the Messiah. When John sent two men to ask Jesus if he really was the Messiah, Jesus replied, "Go back and report to John what you hear and see: The blind receive sight, the lame walk, those who have leprosy are cleansed, the deaf hear, the dead are raised, and the good news is proclaimed to the poor" (Matt. 11:4-5; see also Luke 7:18-22). In other words, Jesus implicitly affirmed his messiahship by citing his (miraculous) service to others, not a takeover of government. He essentially said, "Yes, I am the Messiah. Look at how I've supernaturally healed the disabled and given hope to the poor."

It was a bewildering response. John and his men already knew about Jesus's miracles. That's why they were asking him if he was the Messiah in the first place. Now they wanted confirmation he would also overthrow the Romans and establish a proper earthly kingdom. But Jesus didn't deliver. Instead, he paradoxically affirmed his messiahship while simultaneously rejecting the popular expectation that he would, as the promised Messiah, lead a violent revolution to recapture political power. His answer confirmed that he would liberate and restore God's people, but it also redefined what he would liberate them from and restore them to—from the oppression of disease, disability, poverty, and death to health, abundance, and life, not from political impotence to political dominance.

To view it another way, the miracles Jesus performed throughout his ministry symbolically revealed the nature of his messiahship. He supernaturally cured infirmities, exorcised demons, and tamed nature. He did not supernaturally restore Israel's earthly empire. Despite possessing the ability to call down twelve legions of angels from heaven at any time, he didn't even employ supernatural violence to defend himself from being tortured to death on a cross.[11] Jesus used his powers to heal and redeem, not to destroy and control.

To summarize Jesus's relationship with political power, he unequivocally rejected it as a means of advancing God's kingdom on earth. He never wielded it or even pursued it. When offered it, he rejected and rebuked it, even fleeing from it on one occasion. Likewise, he never instructed his followers to use it, not even to promote social justice, advance the common good, or make the world safe for democracy. Instead, he commanded them not to use it and condemned them when they sought it. Jesus did everything he could to avoid and rebuff political power, for himself and his followers.

The exercise of political power consists of forcing your will, your way of life, on others. Jesus didn't force his on anyone, ever. Instead, he invited them to accept it voluntarily. And even then, he warned them against doing so before counting the cost, before comprehending just how much self-sacrifice it would require.[12] He also instructed his followers not to force the gospel on anyone: "If anyone will not welcome you or listen to your words, leave that home or town and shake the dust off your feet" (Matt. 10:14).

Jesus advanced God's kingdom on earth by embodying it, not by coercively imposing it. He fought injustice through example, not control. Instead of using political power to maintain social order, ensure history turns out right, or accomplish the myriad of other tasks we think we need to use government for, he humbly, patiently, and obediently entrusted such things to God. Despite all the material good he could have accomplished with political power, Jesus remained faithful to his father by resisting the *temptation* to use it, not by employing it more effectively or more justly than others.

Jesus's kingship is defined not by his better use of political power but by his renunciation of political power, by his refusal to "lord" over others like the "rulers of the Gentiles." He controlled no territory, commanded no army, and enforced no laws. As Zahnd puts it, "Caesar is a crucifying king who reigns by force. Christ is the crucified king who reigns without force."[13] Or as Napoleon reportedly said, "Alexander, Caesar, Charlemagne, and I myself have founded great empires. But our empires were founded on force. Jesus alone founded His empire on love."

Again, this is precisely the point at which Jesus differs from the Zealots. They believed in beating the world at its own game (of violence), but Jesus believes in playing a different game, an entirely nonviolent one. He believes in forgoing the tactics of politics in favor of the strategies of love.

A Key Distinction

Jesus declared that nonviolence is a key distinction between his kingdom and all other earthly kingdoms. After he had been arrested and was being questioned by Pilate, a Roman governor, Jesus explained, "My kingdom is not of this world. If it were, my servants would fight to prevent my arrest by the Jewish leaders. But now my kingdom is from another place" (John 18:36).

Jesus's statement is often misinterpreted as proclaiming that his kingdom is not in this world or not for this world, that it is an otherworldly kingdom, one that is merely spiritual, internal, or personal and not pragmatically relevant in the here and now. But that's not what he said. He claimed his kingdom is not *of* this world. He did not say it is not *in* or not *for* this world. Likewise, he said it is *from* another place, not that it is *at* another place. There's a difference. A big one.

The word *of* indicates a different character or nature, not a different objective or location. Had Jesus wanted to reveal that his kingdom has a different objective, he would have said it is not *for* this world. Likewise, the word *from* indicates Jesus's kingdom is here now but originated from a different place, not that it is currently in a different place. Had Jesus wanted to indicate that, he would have said it is not *in* this world. He didn't.

We must not interpret this passage through escapist goggles, which erroneously make Christianity appear to be about individuals making it to heaven—about them escaping earth, avoiding hell, and achieving eternal bliss when they die. As discussed in Chapter 5, Jesus came to earth for the very purpose of establishing God's kingdom "*on earth* as it is in heaven" (Matt. 6:10).

There's no doubt Jesus's kingdom is not *from* this world or *of* this world, but there's also no doubt that it is *in* this world and *for* this world.

So what was Jesus trying to communicate in this passage? Two things. First, he was asserting that his kingdom has a fundamentally different nature than all the other kingdoms of the world: "My kingdom is not *of* this world." Second, he was explaining how it is different: "If it were [of this world], my servants would fight to prevent my arrest by the Jewish leaders."

In other words, Jesus was declaring nonviolence to be a distinguishing characteristic of his earthly kingdom. He was saying that his kingdom is not a traditional, secular, violence-based, earthly kingdom, that it doesn't use force to establish itself, grow itself, or defend itself. He was pointing out that government is force, that earthly kingdoms are defined by their ability and willingness to coerce and fight, but that his kingdom is precisely the opposite—it is defined by its non-forcefulness and its unwillingness to fight. He was reiterating that the Gentile rulers lord over others, but that he and his followers don't.

Had Jesus stopped speaking after stating that his kingdom is not of this world, he could have meant it was different in any number of ways. But he didn't. He kept talking and plainly explained how it differs: nonviolence.

However, in saying that his kingdom is not of this world because his followers do not fight, Jesus wasn't proclaiming that his kingdom is nonpolitical. He was explaining *how* it is political.

Nor was Jesus correcting the mistaken belief that his kingdom is for this world or in this world when it isn't. He was correcting the mistaken belief that his kingdom employs violence when it doesn't. After all, he made the statement while standing in front of a Roman governor on charges of insurrection. And apparently even Pilate understood and accepted Jesus's distinction. He told the Jews he saw no basis for charging Jesus, no evidence that he was a violent rebel.[14]

Furthermore, not only did Jesus reiterate the nonviolent nature of his kingdom in this passage, he also told the world how to identify his true followers: by their refusal to fight. This wasn't the first time he singled out nonviolence as a distinctive Christian characteristic; this was just his most explicit and public one. Because we know

Christlike love is wholly nonviolent, he implicitly proclaimed the same thing when he had previously told his disciples, "As I have loved you, so you must love one another. By this everyone will know that you are my disciples, if you love one another" (John 13:34-35).

In fact, when we read the rest of the New Testament with an eye toward the ethics of violence, nonviolence emerges over and over again as an indispensable attribute of discipleship. For example, consider again the types of weapons used in God's kingdom. Paul wrote, "The weapons we fight with are not the weapons of the world" (2 Cor. 10:4). We battle evil by putting on "the full armor of God," which consists of "the belt of truth … the breastplate of righteousness … the shield of faith … the helmet of salvation and the sword of the Spirit, which is the word of God" (Eph. 6:14-17). We wear "faith and love as a breastplate, and the hope of salvation as a helmet" (1 Thess. 5:8).

Such weapons are markedly nonviolent. We wield love, faith, and truth, not clubs, machine guns, or tanks. Instead of shooting bullets, we disperse kindness. We fight by praying, forgiving, serving, speaking the truth, and imitating Jesus—not by employing force, whether personal or political.

Yes, we are soldiers who engage in combat and wage war, but we do so in a manner that is fundamentally different from that of the world.[15] We do so nonviolently. "So let us put aside the deeds of darkness and put on the armor of light," as Paul encouraged (Rom. 13:12). Let us become "instruments of righteousness," not violence (Rom. 6:13).

Also consider the traits attributed to those who inhabit God's kingdom. The Bible describes them as people who obey God's commands, who love him, who become like children, who are persecuted because of righteousness, who serve others, who take care of the poor, sick, and imprisoned, who are forgiving, humble, meek, and merciful, and who add goodness, knowledge, self-control, perseverance, godliness, mutual affection, and love to their faith.[16] Not only are these attributes wholly nonviolent, they are the antithesis of violence.

On the other hand, the Bible says that those who give into the temptations of the flesh—theft, murder, sexual immorality, adultery, impurity, debauchery, idolatry, witchcraft, hatred, discord, jealousy, anger, selfish ambition, dissensions, factions, envy, greed, drunkenness, orgies, falsehood, etc.—will not inhabit God's kingdom.[17] As Paul wrote, "The mind governed by the flesh is hostile to God; it does not submit to God's law, nor can it do so" (Rom. 8:7). Is there anything fleshier than violence?

On two occasions, Jesus condemned the attempts of violent people to integrate themselves into God's kingdom. He told a crowd, "From the days of John the Baptist until now, the kingdom of heaven has been subjected to violence, and violent people have been raiding it" (Matt. 11:12).[18] He later told his disciples, "The Law and the Prophets were proclaimed until John. Since that time, the good news of the kingdom of God is being preached, and everyone is forcing their way into it" (Luke 16:16). As N. T. Wright explains, "men of violence were trying to muscle their way into the act" and Jesus wanted nothing to do with them.[19]

There's a reason why Jesus reorganized God's followers from a nation into a church. Nations require violence. To exist, they need criminal laws, national defense policies, and armed men to enforce them. By their nature, they have order to maintain, territory to protect, and national sovereignty to preserve. But transnational, interethnic, nongovernmental, geographically dispersed organizations (like the universal church) do not. People living as exiles and foreigners on earth do not. People who are called to take the gospel to all nations and to be the salt and light of the entire world—and to do so as sheep among wolves—do not. They need not acquire or control land, and therefore they need not use violence.

By denationalizing God's followers, Jesus freed us to be known by our nonviolence.[20]

We could go on, but you get the point. Beginning with Jesus, everything in the Bible suggests that the citizens of God's kingdom are distinguishable from the citizens of all other earthly kingdoms by their *nonuse* of violence, not by their more moral, more benevolent, more just, or more effective use of violence.

The Incomprehensible King

Jesus was so nonviolent, so unlike all other earthly kings, that everyone rejected his messiahship—at least initially.

The Israelites expected a traditional earthly king, one who would use violence to conquer and then rule their enemies. Moreover, like all fallen humans, they *wanted* such a king. They yearned to restore their national sovereignty, regain political power, and revive their national ambitions. And they sought a Messiah who could accomplish such things.

But Jesus didn't deliver. He gathered no army, acquired no political power, recaptured no territory, and killed no enemies. He didn't even attempt to do so. Instead, he purposefully avoided using physical force of any kind.

The Israelites couldn't understand it. How could someone be nonviolent and still be king? A kingdom without violence was akin to a lake without water. A nonviolent king was an oxymoron, like a square circle or a black sun. It was nonsensical. To be king meant to use violence. Whoever could best wield and control violence got to rule. That's just how it worked.

So the Israelites rejected Jesus. Not only did his nonviolence violate their sense of justice and offend their national ego, it was so paradoxical, so unrealistic, so far outside their worldview they couldn't comprehend it.[21] They believed they knew what it took to be God's promised Messiah, and nonviolent Jesus simply didn't measure up. As Benjamin L. Corey describes it, "They expected a warrior Messiah who would free them from Roman oppression, but all they got was an itinerant preacher who told them to love and serve their enemies."[22]

Even Jesus's disciples initially rejected the notion of a nonviolent Messiah who would allow his enemies to kill him. He had to gradually prepare them to view his self-sacrificial death not as a failure but as a victory, as the way his kingdom engages and overcomes its enemies. When he first told them he was the Messiah, he tied his messiahship to what he would endure on the cross.[23] Their instinctual reaction was disbelief and denial, as exemplified by Peter in the passage discussed earlier.[24] So from that day on, the Bible tells us, Jesus began explaining to them that he would have to suffer, die, and rise again.[25]

John the Baptist, the prophet tasked with preparing God's people for the arrival of his promised Messiah, apparently experienced the same initial doubt about Jesus. In prison for proclaiming the imminent arrival of the messianic revolution, but having seen no evidence that Jesus was preparing to recapture the throne, he sent two men to ask him if he really was the Messiah.[26] Because Jesus wasn't doing kingly things, John was having a hard time seeing how he could be the one who would reestablish God's kingdom on earth. (Of course, as we saw above, Jesus confirmed he was, but instead of reassuring John that a violent rebellion was at hand, he pointed him to his miraculous acts of healing and restoration.)

As John's gospel summarizes, Jesus "came to that which was his own, but his own did not receive him" (John 1:11). "For even his own brothers did not believe in him" (7:5).

In hindsight, everyone's nonviolence-related rejection of Jesus as the Messiah was understandable. In the world's terms, he was a failed king, if he even qualified to be called a king. No one anticipated, or wanted, a suffering servant Messiah, one who would end up nailed to a cross. The scriptural, historical, and national precedent (as contained in the Old Testament) largely supported the expectation of a typical earthly king who would conquer and reign through violence and political power.

Only after the resurrection was Jesus's nonviolent kingship comprehensible. It took a demonstration of Jesus's supernatural power over death to convince humans that he willingly chose the way of nonviolent, self-sacrificial love. Without the resurrection, the crucifixion was a failure. With it, it was—and can be understood as—a victory.

Kingship Redefined

By rejecting violence in all of its forms, including political power, Jesus redefined kingship. He denationalized, demilitarized, and de-violenced it. He became, to borrow N. T. Wright's description, a "true king," not the "ordinary, shabby, second-rate sort" humans had become accustomed to.[27] This is why he was rejected. Humans "were looking for a builder to construct the home they thought they wanted, but he was the architect, coming with a new plan that would give them everything they needed, but within quite a new framework."[28] Jesus did not come to earth to be a better version of a typical earthly ruler. "He was the king all right, but he had come to redefine kingship itself around his own work, his own mission, his own fate."²⁹

Best of all, Jesus's unique kingship is defined by love. He ascended to the throne through love and he reigns through love. Praise be to God.

---

¹ This is from N.T. Wright's translation of the New Testament: *The Kingdom New Testament: A Contemporary Translation* (Kindle Locations 799-800).

² Gregory A. Boyd, *The Myth of a Christian Religion: Losing Your Religion for the Beauty of a Revolution* (Zondervan, 2009), 313, Kindle.

³ John 12:31; 14:30; 16:11; 2 Cor. 4:4; 1 John 5:19.

⁴ Gregory A. Boyd, *A Faith Not Worth Fighting For: Addressing Commonly Asked Questions about Christian Nonviolence* (The Peaceable Kingdom Series), ed. Tripp York and Justin Bronson Barringer (Cascade Books, 2012), 2305, Kindle.

⁵ For additional examples, see Matt. 18:4, 19:30, and Luke 9:48.

⁶ For a few examples, see 1 Pet. 2:16; 4:10; 5:1-5; Gal. 5:13; 1 Cor. 9:19; Eph. 5:21; Phil. 2:3-8; Rom. 12:1; 13:1; and Titus 3:1-2.

⁷ See Boyd's Foreword in Keith Giles' *Jesus Untangled: Crucifying Our Politics to Pledge Allegiance to the Lamb* (Quoir, 2017), 148, Kindle.

⁸ Matt. 8:1-4; 9:30; 12:16; 16:13-25; 17:9; Mark 1:34, 40-45; 3:12; 5:43; 8:26-35; 9:9; Luke 4:41; 5:12-16; 8:56; 9:18-24.

⁹ Matt. 16:13-25; Mark 8:27-35; Luke 9:18-24.

¹⁰ Matt. 21:1-11; Mark 11:1-10; Luke 19:28-38; John 12:12-16.

¹¹ Matt. 26:52-53. For another example of such supernatural restraint, see Luke 9:51-56 wherein Jesus rebuked his followers' request to "call fire down from heaven to destroy" a group of his enemies.

¹² For example, see Luke 14:25-33.

¹³ Brian Zahnd, *Water to Wine: Some of My Story* (Spello Press, 2016), 1715, Kindle.

¹⁴ John 18:38.

¹⁵ 2 Cor. 10:3.

¹⁶ Matt. 5:3-10,19-20; 7:21; 18:3-4, 23-35; 19:14, 17; 20:26; 25:34-36; James 2:5; Mark 10:15-19; Luke 18:16-17; 2 Pet. 1:5-11; 2 Thess. 1:3-10.

¹⁷ Gal. 5:16-21; Eph. 5:5; 1 Cor. 6:9-11; Rev. 22:15; Matt. 19:16-19.

¹⁸ The NIV notes that "has been subjected to violence" can also be interpreted as "has been forcefully advancing."

¹⁹ N. T. Wright, *Simply Jesus*, 2524.

[20] For a more thorough explanation of Jesus's denationalization of God's followers and its nonviolence implications, see Chapters 3 and 4 in my book *The Old Testament Case for Nonviolence.*

[21] Many people today, Jews and non-Jews alike, still reject Jesus's nonviolent kingship for these same reasons.

[22] Benjamin L. Corey, *Undiluted: Rediscovering the Radical Message of Jesus* (Destiny Image, 2014), 1678, Kindle.

[23] Matt. 16:13-25; Mark 8:27-35; Luke 9:18-24.

[24] Matt. 16:13-25; Mark 8:27-35.

[25] Matt. 16:13-25; 17:9, 12, 23; 20:18-19; Mark 8:27-35; 9:12, 31; 10:34; Luke 9:18-24; 17:25; 24:7.

[26] Matt 11:2-3; Luke 7:18-20.

[27] N. T. Wright, *Simply Jesus*, 193.

[28] Ibid.

[29] Ibid., 212.

CHAPTER 9

NONVIOLENCE INCARNATE

Jesus was completely pacifistic, nonviolent from every angle. He arrived on earth in the form of a poor, humble, working-class commoner, not a mighty warrior or great king. He adopted the lifestyle of an itinerant servant and preacher, not a violent revolutionary or political power broker. Instead of teaching his followers how to use violence more morally or justly, he instructed them not to use it at all, not even against their enemies or in defense of their own lives. Although he lived during a time of great injustice and had the opportunity to employ violence for "good," he rejected it in all its forms, personal and political. In fact, if anyone has ever been justified in using violence to do God's will, it was Jesus. Yet he wholeheartedly, unequivocally, and uncompromisingly rejected it as a means of advancing God's kingdom on earth. Instead, he fought and conquered evil by absorbing violence, not by inflicting or controlling it. He was willing to die for God's kingdom, but not willing to kill for it.

Everything about Jesus—his actions, commands, sermons, kingship, and death—promoted nonviolence. He prophesied about it, embodied it, taught it, and modeled it. He was, as Gandhi put it, "nonviolence par excellence."[1]

The existence of a handful of commonly misinterpreted statements doesn't negate Jesus's radical pacifism. Neither does a single symbolic act involving a minimal amount of reactive physical force against a few animals and some furniture. Ditto for a few violent analogies, metaphors, and parables—to preach peace by occasionally using the terminology of war is not to condone war.

Jesus himself sarcastically questioned those who interpreted him as anything other than thoroughly pacifistic. When the armed crowd came to arrest him in the Garden of Gethsemane, he asked, "Am I leading a rebellion that you have come out with swords and clubs to capture me? Every day I sat in the temple courts teaching, and you did not arrest me" (Matt. 26:55). Only those who severely misunderstood him would bring an armed mob to arrest the always-publicly-accessible poster child of nonviolence, the guy whose entire way of life exuded an aversion to violent resistance.

Attempts to characterize Jesus as anything but entirely nonviolent can get rather silly rather quickly. We have to take a handful of minor passages (roughly only 2% of all the passages that describe Jesus's life), misinterpret them into passages that advocate violence, and then allow them to override everything else Jesus said and did (the other 98%). We have to turn Jesus's violent metaphors, analogies, and parables into direct and literal ethical instructions, while turning his direct and literal ethical instructions into non-ethically-related hyperbole. We must conclude that a certain few incidents, in which the ethics of violence weren't even at issue, not only support violence but also trump all the other, more numerous incidents in which violence *was* at issue and was clearly condemned. To put it bluntly, we have to miss the forest for the trees and then apply a non-contextual, proof-texting analysis to the trees.

Such an interpretive approach can make the Bible support almost anything. For example, by pulling a bunch of verses out of context, stringing them together, and then adding in a few fallacious arguments from silence, we can even make a "biblical" case for slavery. In the Old Testament, God explicitly sanctioned slavery: "From [the surrounding nations] you may buy slaves. You may also buy some of the temporary residents living among you and members of their clans born in your country, and they will become your property. You can bequeath them to your children as inherited property and can make them slaves for life" (Lev. 25:44-46). Then in the New Testament, Jesus never specifically condemned slavery and used many slavery analogies and parables.[2] One of his parables even implies that beating a slave is acceptable.[3] Furthermore, on many occasions, Paul commanded slaves to obey their masters.[4] So did Peter, adding that even harsh masters should be obeyed.[5] Paul also took the ownership of slaves by Christians for granted, specifically instructing slaves to obey "believing masters" (1 Tim. 6:2). In fact, according to the book of Philemon, Paul sent an escaped slave back to his Christian slave owner, telling the owner that he should free the slave but that ultimately it was his choice.

Read in isolation, the implication of these verses is clear: God condones and possibly even encourages slavery. But read in the context of everything else the Bible says, including its other verses about slavery, such a conclusion is preposterous. As I and many others are fond of saying when it comes to biblical interpretation, context is key.[6]

In our case, the overwhelming weight of the contextual evidence is clear: Jesus was a pacifist. Such a conclusion is rooted in the heart of his teachings, sermons, actions, and death, while the idea of a violent Jesus is built upon a handful of poorly interpreted, relatively peripheral passages.

Called to Pacifism

The Bible calls us to obey and mimic Jesus. His is *the* standard of Christian conduct, the perfect human example of how to advance God's kingdom on earth. To the extent that we live like and obey him, we fulfill our Christian duty and purpose. To the extent that we don't, we fall short.

Consequently, nonviolence is an essential component of Christian ethics, an indispensable aspect of discipleship. For those who seek to be Christlike, violence is not an option. Jesus crucified its moral acceptability. He did and taught everything God wants us to do, and he never employed or taught violence. Therefore, if we are to carry Jesus's ethical torch, nonviolence must be as integral to our lives as it was to his. After all, as Zahnd points out, "Jesus did not renounce the way of violence for the way of peace so that we could renounce the way of peace for the way of violence."[7]

This is how Jesus's disciples interpreted and obeyed him. They viewed pacifism as the logical conclusion to taking him seriously. After his death, they continued preaching nonviolence and they willingly suffered violence rather than use it themselves. Most of them even died a martyr's death, just like Jesus. The apostle Paul provides a powerful example. Upon conversion, he made one of history's most dramatic ethical pivots—from a professional user of violence to a complete non-user of nonviolence, one who was eventually beheaded for his beliefs. Similarly, for about the first three hundred years of its existence, the church followed suit, remaining pacifistic until it gained political power under Constantine.

If nonviolence isn't a key element of Christlikeness, what was the point of Jesus's uncompromising pacifism? Why was he so perfectly, so totally and completely, so thoroughly and comprehensively nonviolent? Even if his earthly mission prevented him from using violence to avoid dying on a cross, why didn't he at least leave us with a few instructions on how to employ it Christianly, or otherwise tone down his antiviolence rhetoric?

The only way to Christianize violence is to remove the Christ from *Christian* ethics. To conclude that violence can be Christian, we have to reject the belief that an action is Christian insofar as it comports with Jesus's teachings and example. We have to discard the biblical Jesus as our standard and replace him with something else, something of our own making. Unfortunately, many Christians do just that. As Gandhi observed, "The only people on earth who do not see Christ and his teachings as nonviolent are Christians."[8] Ouch.

But What About ...?

"Okay," you might be thinking, "Jesus was a pacifist and taught nonviolence. But what does this mean for our everyday lives? Isn't total pacifism unrealistic in a fallen world? What if someone breaks into my house and tries to murder my spouse and kids? Don't I have a moral duty to protect them, even with violence if necessary? And what about law and order? What would happen to society if government didn't use violence to restrain evildoers? For that matter, what about Hitler?"

These are good and necessary questions, ones that deserve studied and thorough answers, which I'm hoping to take a stab at in another book. But before we can have a productive discussion about how to apply Jesus's ethical instructions as a Christian community, we must first identify, define, and agree on what those ethical instructions are. That's what this book has been about. Hopefully it has moved the ball farther down that field. Hopefully, for you, the issue has evolved from "Did Jesus teach and embody pacifism?" to "How do we apply Jesus's pacifism in our everyday lives, both private and public?"

Just as the first step to fixing any personal problem is admitting you have one, the first step to ending Christian violence is admitting that Jesus embodied and advocated pacifism.

---

[1] M. K. Gandhi, *Non-Violence in Peace and War*, Volume II (Ahmedabad: Navajivan Publishing House, 1948), 16.

[2] Matt. 18:21-35; 20:20-28; 24:36-51.

[3] Luke 12:47.

[4] Eph. 6:5; Col. 3:22; Titus 2:9-10.

[5] 1 Pet. 2:18.

[6] Unfortunately, if someone refuses to consider the basic elements of responsible textual interpretation (e.g., the literary, historical, cultural, biblical, and theological contexts), there's simply no refuting their arguments.

[7] Brian Zahnd, *A Farewell to Mars: An Evangelical Pastor's Journey Toward the Biblical Gospel of Peace* (David C. Cook, 2014), 1973, Kindle.

[8] Walter Wink, *Engaging the Powers: Discernment and Resistance in a World of Domination* (Minneapolis, MN: Fortress Press, 1992), 216.

AUTHOR'S NOTE

First, thank you for reading my book! I pray it has been a blessing.

Second, a little bit about me. I'm a reader, writer, and attorney with a passion for exploring God's beauty and brilliance. I live in Oklahoma City with my bride and three children. If you'd like to learn more or sign up to be notified of future books, new blog posts, and other goodies, please visit www.matthewcurtisfleischer.com. You can also find me on Facebook or on Twitter at @MatthewCurtisF.

Lastly, if you would like to help this book reach a wider audience, please consider (1) leaving a review on Amazon, Goodreads, or anywhere else readers visit and (2) mentioning it on social media. I'd be honored to have your help. Thank you!

Sincerely,
Matthew

MatthewCurtisFleischer@gmail.com

Special thanks to my bride Nicole, Pastor Aaron Bolerjack, Dr. Marty Alan Michelson, and theologian extraordinaire Greg Boyd, each of whom generously made invaluable contributions to this book.

Manufactured by Amazon.ca
Bolton, ON